Jeff & Barbara Gall
Running and Fat Burning

Jeff and Barbara Galloway

Running and Fat Burning for Women

Meyer & Meyer Sport

British Library Cataloguing in Publication Data
A catalogue record for this book is available from the British Library

Jeff and Barbara Galloway: Running and Fat Burning for Women
Maidenhead: Meyer & Meyer Sport (UK) Ltd., 2009
ISBN 978-1-84126-243-7

© 2009 by Meyer & Meyer Sport (UK) Ltd.
Adelaide, Auckland, Budapest, Cape Town, Graz, Indianapolis,
Maidenhead, New York, Olten (CH), Singapore, Toronto
Member of the World
Sport Publishers' Association (WSPA)
www.w-s-p-a.org
Printed and bound by: B.O.S.S Druck und Medien GmbH, Germany
ISBN 978-1-84126-243-7
E-Mail: verlag@m-m-sports.com
www.m-m-sports.com

CONTENTS

Read This First!

By Barbara Galloway

I had heard the flight attendant's speech hundreds of times but one statement never felt quite right. It's the part about using the oxygen mask in an emergency when you're with a child who is dependent upon you. It's hard for me to think about taking oxygen myself before giving it to a child.

In our society, women tend to be the caregivers. We also like to avoid conflict by going with the patterns of the social group—even when we know that changing would improve quality of health. We want our family members and friends to be comfortable and avoid discomfort. Our instincts are to put the others first and neglect ourselves.

This is not working. A greater percentage of today's children are severely overweight or obese than at any time in history. The experts who study these trends say that due to the increase in type two diabetes alone, brought on by fatness, this current generation of kids will be the first generation of Americans which will not outlive their parents. The worse part is that the quality of life for our children will deteriorate significantly because they are overweight.

It's clear from the research that children tend to pick up lifestyle practices from their mothers more than any other influence. But more women are severely overweight today than at any time in history. It's time to take the oxygen mask. Even if you don't have children, you can be a prime force in helping friends and family members to feel better, and avoid long-term debilitating diseases. For example, every person who trains for an event like the National Marathon to Fight Breast Cancer influences at least 20 people to improve their health.

We know that we should exercise a bit more, and should eat a bit better. But the kids/spouse/friends love french fries, and video games/TV. We also tend to feel guilty for spending time to exercise when there is so much to do. Grab the oxygen mask and inhale.

It's stressful to start an exercise program, to change eating habits, and especially to admit that our lifestyle has been off track for years. But exercise will release much of the stress. Furthermore, each one of us is capable of change and can influence others to do so without preaching. You can take more control over your health, vitality, and produce a better attitude. Because you are breathing the oxygen from the mask, you are empowered to be a better Mom, co-worker, sister, daughter, and friend.

This book has successful plans for integrating gentle uplifting exercise, and energizing healthy food, into your life. Thousands of women have taken this path before you and are experiencing the best years of their lives. But many women start and stop a fat burning program several times before they are "ready" to do so. This doesn't mean that the person doesn't have the internal strength to make it happen. In our experience, the degree of success in adapting to the new lifestyle depends upon an intuitive awareness similar to the "readiness" in a child before reading can be learned. Women must be ready to blend body, mind and spirit into a commitment to the enjoyment of regular exercise and energizing food choices.

If you are having trouble with the readiness issue, we recommend the book CHANGING FOR GOOD (James Prochaska, John Norcross, Carlo DiClemente). Inside is a six stage program for overcoming bad habits and moving forward.

When you are ready, take the oxygen mask, inhale, and then pass it around.

Jennifer shifted priorities and lost 100 pounds while making the lifestyle transition from school to work-marriage-kids, Jennifer put everyone else first and gained 100 pounds. The day after 9-11-01 when our whole nation was rethinking life, Jennifer decided to lose that poundage through diet and exercise. As a child, she hated running. But as the daughter of a marathoner, she knew that running was a very efficient fat burner. She laced up her sneakers, left the kids with hubby and ran to the mailbox. The 7 year journey included a complicated pregnancy and post partum, a serious car accident, learning to love running and then finishing the 2008 Tom King Half Marathon in 2:04. One month before this race Jennifer had celebrated losing the 100 pounds which was her 2001 vision. "I am living proof that you don't have to be built like an Olympian to reap the benefits of running."

You're in Control!

The only requirement to start: The desire to become more active and manage food portions

- The methods in this book have helped women burn off 10, 20, 50 and even more than 100 pounds—AND KEEP IT OFF!
- You only need to walk to burn significant fat—or choose your own exercises.
- There are an unlimited number of calories you can burn with gentle exercise.
- You don't have to give up chocolate or your glass of wine.
- You have the power inside to take responsibility for your eating and your exercise.
- Have patience—it took years to accumulate fat, and it's best to burn it off gradually.
- You're establishing positive relationships with food and exercise.
- This program gives you control over motivation, desire to exercise, eating patterns, and your attitude.

This is not a "diet" book. Restrictive diets almost never work. The exercise can be done mostly in shorter segments, inserted into busy days—without aches and pains. The food we recommend is easy to find and easy to prepare. You don't have to join a health club, hire a personal trainer, enroll in a weight loss program or buy expensive food or exercise equipment.

Food is your friend when you manage your eating. With our plan you will be eating frequently. Infusing exercise and eating into your day gives you more vitality all day long, physically and mentally. Frequent snacks and extra walking steps keep your metabolism revved into a fat burning furnace that burns day and night.

When exercising at the right effort level, body, mind, and spirit come together to produce a feeling of great satisfaction. Once you have the right balance, you won't want to miss a single enhancing workout. More powerful than body shape improvement or weight reduction is the sense of achievement and control. When paced correctly and done regularly, you'll enjoy the feeling of exertion during and after exercise. Many who get "hooked" on exercise find unexpected psychological strength to make other positive changes in their life.

- Exercisers have restorative time to themselves
- The stress release from exercise is immediate and empowering
- Exercise allows you to be in control—no need for excuses
- The information in this book is given as coaching advice—from two exercisers to others. For medical advice or technical nutritional information see medical authorities and registered dietitians.

So prepare to feel better about yourself, with more energy to enjoy life. You can do it!

The Three Part Plan
- You are in control of the process.
- You have the power to take responsibility for your eating and your exercise.
- Have patience and don't give up.
- Enjoyment of exercise is the key.

- You are in command of a "calorie budget", as you add gentle movement to your daily activities.

Part One: Eating with a purpose. Starting on page 66, you'll be introduced to food that is easily available, most of which can be prepared quickly. You'll see how to set up your eating plan to gain control over the calorie balance each day, as well as the vitamins, minerals, and other nutritional ingredients you need each day. Websites are great tools because you'll learn portion control—while you account for needed nutrients. You'll also learn whether you're getting the nutrients you need and then adjust with an eating plan to compensate if needed.

Part Two: Creating your fat burning furnace. By gradually increasing a long walk or run-walk, or your longer workouts of choice each week, you will train thousands of muscle cells to burn more fat—not only while exercising. Once adapted to fat burning, these muscle cells will burn more fat when you're sitting and walking around—even at night when asleep!

Part Three: Taking more steps per day. Get a step counter and increase the number of steps taken per day. As you do your daily activities, fill up the "dead time" when you would be sitting, by walking segments of 5-10 minutes at a time. Extra steps, in segments of 500-2000 do not tend to increase appetite—but they burn fat all day long.

Fat burning not weight loss While the scales are an important tool, you cannot be obsessed about daily changes in weight. Water fluctuations in your body will have you up one day, down the next. As you adjust your daily exertions and your many energizing meals you can control the process through real fat burnoff. The scales will continue to fluctuate somewhat, but the overall fat level can be reduced—even if the "daily scales report" is a bit higher on some days.

Good weight vs. bad weight Muscle mass that is used during exercise, regularly, weighs more than an equivalent mass of untrained muscle fibers. When women begin exercising, they often experience a slight weight gain as the muscle adapts in many ways: extra storage for fuel, more water for cooling off and processing energy, and increased blood volume for delivery of oxygen and withdrawal of waste products. Your muscles are being transformed into vibrant athletic muscles that can burn a lot of fat often with less fatigue than you are experiencing now.

A Positive Relationship with Food

By Barbara Galloway

"Every woman is capable of having a positive relationship with energizing food."

- Your relationship with food is crucial for fat burning.
- A negative relationship means eating to make you feel better.
- A positive relationship means managing your food choices so that you have energy all day long.
- Each day you have a budget of calories.
- Energy is maintained by eating more often: 6-8 times a day.
- You'll choose snacks that leave you satisfied because nutrients are balanced.
- Each snack has a purpose—it's important to get calcium, iron, protein, etc.
- Variety is important. Even if you really like a snack don't eat it all day long, day after day.
- You can still eat and drink some favorites (decadent choices) but they must be budgeted.
- You are in control, and you feel good.

Relationships are important to most women, whether we're relating to men, children, supervisor, food, etc. This desire to have things run smoothly increases stress—and stress can change relationships. Many women deal with stress by eating or drinking foods or beverages that are counterproductive to health and fat burning, especially in the quantities that are consumed. But food and drink, at best, offer only temporary stress relief while they add fat to the body.

In contrast, gentle exercise is a powerful stress eraser that can empower you to make positive changes. In the next chapter we'll explain how this works. Let's look first at the food side of the equation.

YOU can enjoy food that is healthy and energizing. If you don't like certain items now, combine them with other foods, and use some of the great seasoning combinations in recipes from publications such as COOKING LIGHT Magazine. You can learn to like almost anything—and feel better for doing so. To feel good and to maintain a high level of health, you need to eat foods every day that are nutritionally balanced.

YOU have an amazing ability to use the brain to control the stomach. Unfortunately this is usually done during crash diets that set up negative after-effects. We can just as easily program ourselves to eat energizing food, frequently throughout the day, in quantities that don't add fat to our bodies.

YOU can budget calories. Women have to handle budgets constantly. Intake control means putting yourself on a calorie budget. You can still eat the chocolate or drink the wine. You determine how you will use your budget of calories, each day.

YOU can change your relationship with food in a positive direction. You may use food now to drown sorrows, deal with stress or disappointments. But once you realize that this is a bad relationship which you must exit, you are open to a positive one: eating every 2-3 hours, feeling good, finding new foods that you like.

YOU can be in control of the situation. By budgeting calories, planning a little, having good options available and using a "reality check" such as a nutritional website, you can be the captain of your ship.

Changing the relationship can be stressful. Gentle exercise is a powerful tool that can erase/manage an amazing amount of stress. Realize that there will be tough times and don't give up. Millions of women have made the shift and feel so much better.

Stress can be managed. Exercise can help you manage stress in a major way. But unconscious stress buildup can cause the discomfort of little aches and pains to be magnified greatly. To understand this process and manage it, we recommend using the method in the breakthrough book MIND-BODY PRESCRIPTION by Dr. John Sarno.

Feeling better. Once the relationship is working, you feel better throughout the day because you're in control. Reinforce this good feeling by recognizing that your efforts are making a difference. Some women reward themselves at this point with a new outfit—one size down.

More energy to exercise. If you're eating regularly, you will have more energy to do everything, including exercise, by adding more steps to your day.

KEY PRINCIPLES:
- Crucial: Control calorie intake so your exercise can burn off the fat.
- Food is fuel for the next workout or the next 3 hours—keep it flowing in controlled amounts.
- Food contains the building blocks of muscle, bone, organs which must be replaced daily.
- Budget daily totals—through portion control.
- Combining foods so that you feel satisfied with fewer calories consumed.

- Get a "reality check" as you account for the calories every night—eaten and burned (vitamins, minerals, protein, etc.)
- You're in control: Set up your reality check—websites, weight monitoring programs, etc.
- The key to feeling good is managing blood sugar level, which helps you maintain motivation.
- Eat every 2-3 hours.
- Never say never—don't totally abstain from foods you love, ration them.
- Drink water or other low/non-calorie drinks with food and throughout the day to feel satisfied longer.
- Crucial for workout energy: eat 100-300 calories within 30 min of the finish of a workout (composed of 80% simple carb/20% protein).

Final thoughts:

- Sally dieted and lost over 70 pounds in 6 months, but gained back more than that amount within a year.
- Elaine, who exercised, lost 98 pounds and kept it off, 5 years and counting—she learned to enjoy exercise, and the exercise kept the weight from being deposited again.
- Starvation diets show a water weight loss which is quickly added back.
- The exercise/good food relationship creates a behavioral change—you feel good.
- Snacking is OK! But you must choose the right snacks.
- Gain control over the intake side by using one of many good websites. I use www.fitday.com.
- A suggested eating schedule will be offered in this book.

Gentle Exercise Is the Key

"If exercise were a medication it would be the most heavily prescribed in the history of mankind."

- The amount of fat reduction you can make through dieting is limited.
- Exercise is your fat furnace that burns fat all day—and can keep it off.
- When gentle exercise is done correctly you feel better during and afterward.
- Aches and pains from exercise are self induced and can be virtually eliminated.
- Exercising too hard or too long (for you on that day) will often trigger an appetite increase.
- Shorter segments of gentle exercise, like walking, will burn calories without the appetite increase.
- The plan in this book offers exercise options based upon your schedule and lifestyle.
- Your fat burning starts each day with a single step—and each step afterward burns more fat.
- Exercise extends length and quality of life—enjoy your grandchildren with good health.
- See the fat burning training program in this book for a schedule, with tips to make it fun (starting on page 114).

It's a fact that exercise can lower blood pressure, help you manage cholesterol, reduce your chance of cancer, stroke & heart disease, as it extends your lifespan with quality. The best part for me is that exercise makes me feel good about myself—during and after each workout. This is one time in the day when I can get an attitude boost that lasts.

It is also clear that you can burn lots of fat through exercise! Almost every day on the TV talk shows, some woman tells her story: stuck in an obese rut for years, started exercising, controlled the eating, and lost 20, 40, 100 pounds. Read the stories of real people in the "Heroes" section in this book starting on page 44.

YOU CAN DO THIS TOO!

Gentle exercise builds self respect, personal empowerment, and the will to make changes in your life. If you will simply get out and move your feet to get your steps, or go to the gym, the body feels good and your mind focuses better. You may not feel so good before a workout, but there's an after-workout-glow that is energizing and attractive—to the others in your life. Good things happen when you feel good about yourself, and exercise can deliver the honest reward of self-esteem.

- Even a gentle walk for a few minutes makes you feel better than before. You discover many things about yourself that you didn't know:
- That you can get out the door on a busy day and get things done afterward.
- That you can keep going when you didn't think you could.
- That you solve problems (personal, job, family) during and after a workout.
- That you are more productive after a gentle workout, with more energy to do things.
- That you think more clearly when you've exercised at a conservative effort level.

If exercise hurts, you've been doing it wrong, there is something wrong with your orthopedic condition, or you are doing the wrong exercise, for you. The program in this book will make you the captain of your exercise ship. Once you feel the continuing stream of benefits, you will look forward to the next walk, visit to the gym, etc.

Health benefits without weight loss
Even if there is not a weight loss, regular exercise delivers a series of significant health benefits. Studies at the Cooper Clinic,

founded by Dr. Kenneth Cooper in Dallas TX, and other organizations, have shown that even obese people lower their risk factors for heart disease and cancer when they exercise regularly. They also feel better about themselves and accomplish more when regularly exercising.

THE PROGRAM

- One gentle long session a week, gradually building up to 90 min +
- Two workouts of 60 minutes
- 2-3 optional weekly cross-training exercise sessions or gentle walks, of 45 min + (exercise that you enjoy)
- Walking 10,000 steps a day in your daily activities

Exercise does not have to hurt—and should make you feel better. Gentle exertion not only revs up your metabolism so that you feel more energized during the day. The positive attitude effects of gentle exercise leave you feeling better than before you started—and the boost can last for hours.

You're training the muscle cells to burn fat

Exercising at an easy effort will tend to keep you in the "aerobic" or fat burning zone, minute-by minute, hour by hour. Very gentle exercise, done regularly, (even in short segments) will make you fit enough to gradually increase the length of one longer workout a week. As this "long one" increases, you will transform thousands of muscle cells into fat burners. This means that you have increased your daily quantity of fat burned—even when sitting around and when sleeping—than you did before.

You have two types of fuel on board: glycogen and fat

Glycogen is the stored form of carbohydrate and is the primary fuel supply for the brain. It can be used from the beginning of any strenuous exercise as a primary fuel. But this results in an accumulation of a waste product called lactic acid, as it increases your hunger. The supply of glycogen is limited in the human body and must be replenished.

Body fat accumulates from the "direct deposit" of fat eaten in your diet and from excess consumption of carbohydrates and protein. Even very lean individuals have hundreds of miles of fat fuel on board. This energy source is burned by exercisers when they are trained for the type of exertion they are doing and are exercising easily enough.

AEROBIC EXERCISE BURNS FAT—NO HUFFING & PUFFING
- There must be enough oxygen delivered by the blood during exercise, for fat burning to take place.
- When walking, or doing any gentle exercise that does not stress the muscles, the normal flow of blood will deliver enough oxygen to burn fat.
- If you're not huffing and puffing, you're in the aerobic or fat burning zone.
- But when you work out too hard for you, on that day, and you can't carry on a conversation, the muscles are working beyond their current limit. You're out of the fat burning zone.
- The muscles will then shift to glycogen for energy, leaving a lot of waste (lactic acid).
- As your legs fill up with this residue, they get tighter and tighter, and exercise is no fun—muscles hurt.

Hard exercise reduces motivation
The logical circuit of your brain (the left brain) monitors stress and also keeps track of the available supply of glycogen, the fuel source for the brain. As the stress level goes up and the glycogen supply goes down during a hard workout, the right brain triggers a number of negative messages telling you that "it isn't your day", or "this is boring" or "why are you doing this" to preserve it's fuel source.

Hard exercise increases hunger
Hunger increases when the glycogen supply is reduced. Walking at a comfortable pace for short distances requires little glycogen (you're burning primarily fat for fuel). When runners slow down and insert more walk breaks, they tend to reduce hunger. On the

short workout days, many athletes report a reduced appetite response by breaking up the workout into several segments, morning and night. The harder you work out, the hungrier you will tend to be, later in the day or the following day.

Runners, and those who start workouts too hard, burn glycogen during the first 15 minutes

Glycogen is the quick access fuel your body uses during the first quarter hour of strenuous exercise. Those who don't run or who don't work out more than 15 minutes under these conditions, will not fully develop their fat burning capacity. But if you have been depriving yourself of carbohydrates, as when eating a low-carb diet, the glycogen fuel is low and you'll struggle during this warm-up period.

Avoid sore muscles and burn more fat with a very gentle warm-up

It's common to feel good at the beginning of a workout and work out at an exertion level that produces a good bit of lactic acid. If you are huffing and puffing, even at the end of your workout, you have been working too hard, for you, on that day. This waste product builds up in the muscles, leaving them tight afterward, and sore the next day. If you slow the pace of the workout especially during the first 15 minutes, you'll reduce or eliminate the buildup. When in doubt, extend your slow warm-up at the beginning.

From 15 minutes to 45 minutes you'll transition into fat burning

Runners and those who started workouts too fast can reduce the soreness and "gear down" into fat burning by slowing the pace down significantly at the first sign of huffing and puffing. If you are exercising within your capabilities, you will shift into fat burning from the beginning when walking. When running or doing other strenuous exercise gently, you'll start burning fat 15 minutes into your workout, your body starts to break down body fat, and use it as fuel. Fat is actually a more efficient fuel,

producing less waste. This transition continues for the next 30 minutes or so. By the time runners have been exercising within their capabilities for 45-50 minutes, they will be burning mostly fat. With lots of walk breaks or shuffle breaks, and a slow beginning pace, almost anyone can work up to three sessions of 60 minutes within 12 months.

Fat Burning Formula:
Three sessions a week, in the fat burn zone

Even the most un-trained muscles that have only burned glycogen for 50 years can be trained to burn fat under two conditions:

* Gradually increase exercise sessions to 60 minutes each, or more
* Do this regularly: 3 times a week. (best to have no more than two days between sessions)

Maximize fat burning with a 90 minute workout

The endurance session is designed to keep you in the fat burn zone for an extended period. For best results, this should be done every week, and should increase gradually to 90 minutes or more, every other week. If you don't have time for a 90 minute session, you will still burn fat, but won't maximize the fat burning potential.

"By running/walking for 90+ minutes, at a gentle pace, every 14 days, the muscles adapt to burn fat very efficiently. Over time, this means that you have thousands of muscle cells that are burning more fat 24/7, even when you are sitting around at your desk and sleeping at night."

Walk breaks/shuffle breaks allow you to go farther in the fat burn zone without getting tired

When done from the beginning of a walk or run, these periods of reduced exertion allow the muscles to get into the fat-burn zone and stay there, and recover quicker. Read the chapters on these subjects starting on page 158. The number of calories you burn is based upon the number of miles covered, or minutes exercised. Walk breaks/shuffle breaks allow you to cover more distance each day, without being tired all the time. By lowering the exertion level, you will stay in the fat burning zone longer— usually for the whole session. When in doubt, it's best to walk more slowly (runners should insert more walk breaks and slow down the running pace).

To increase the total quantity of fat burned per week

Several short exercise sessions a week can burn fat every day. The secret is to have a series of gentle exercises which you can do throughout the day. You want to enjoy these activities, and they must be easy to insert into your lifestyle.

Walking, for example, offers an almost unlimited opportunity for burning fat, while allowing you to feel better the rest of the day. Instead of sitting down while you are watching kids, waiting for a meeting or appointment, WALK! The steps add up.

Your gentle exercise plan is waiting for you in the "Exercise Is FUN" section (starting on page 105).

Women's Issues

Women-Specific Exercise Issues
Heroes: Women Like You Who Have Burned It Off
Fabulously Full-Figured
Family & Friend Issues
Getting Kids or Adults Into Exercise

Women-Specific Exercise Issues

By Barbara Galloway

While most of the principles of physiology and training apply to men and women alike, there are some significant gender differences. Men tend to have larger and stronger muscles, more testosterone and stronger bones than women. Women have wider/flexible hips, and greater fat storage. After coaching many women for over 30 years, we've found that women exercisers have more patience, tend to be more aware of the changes (especially hormonal) in their bodies, place great value in long term health and are more likely to back off before the aches become injuries. In this chapter we will address the problems that only women face—with some resources.

Movement of internal organs

There is no evidence that walking or even running will cause the internal organs to move around and be damaged. Experts believe that our ancient ancestors regularly covered thousands of miles every year—probably more than most Olympic athletes today. Some who study this period of primitive human history believe that women made these constant journeys while pregnant and when carrying young children.

Breast Issues

Some women are concerned that strenuous exercise can break down breast tissue. I've seen no evidence for this in any research or noted by any expert in this field. There are support and chaffing issues which are managed daily by millions of women exercisers. Larger breasted women may have a tendency to walk or run with a slight forward lean which can produce lower back and neck muscle fatigue and pain. The postural muscle exercises suggested in this book can help in managing this problem.

Bras

This piece of exercise equipment is just as important as shoes for comfort and exercise enjoyment for most women. If the shoes and bra are not selected for your specific needs, you won't be very comfortable and can be miserable. You will gain a great deal of control over your comfort during exercise when you take as much time as necessary to select the model that supports you best, and fits your body. Be prepared to pay significantly more than you would pay for your everyday bra. Remember that bras usually last a lot longer than shoes.

- There are a growing number of bras designed for specific types of exercise, based upon cup size. Enell, Moving Comfort, Champion, and Nike are just a few of the brands.
- Many of the well-constructed "workout bras" are not supportive or comfortable for some women. The elastic in these products (for twisting and extraneous motion in tennis, pilates, etc.) allows for significant bouncing and stress when walking at a brisk pace, or running.
- Comfort: Look first at the fibers next to your body. The microfibers can move moisture away from your skin. This can greatly reduce chaffing (see next section).

  - A & B Cups: Women who wear these sizes can often find support with an elastic compression bra. There will still be some movement during exercise, and sometimes some skin irritation (particularly during long workouts) but this is usually minimal (see the next section on chaffing).
  - C, D & E Cups: Compression bras don't work. Look for brands that have cup sizing, and straps that have minimal or no elastic. Strap placement will differ among individuals—so try on a variety of bras to find the configuration that matches up with your body. If you receive pressure on the shoulders, where the straps press down, padded straps can help. Many large breasted women have reported success with the Enell brand and the Fiona model from Moving Comfort. Champion has a seamless underbra with underwire that has also been successful.

Due to hormone fluctuations, many women find that their breasts are more sensitive at certain times of the month than others. A more supportive bra may provide more comfort when this occurs.

BRA FITTING

- Overall, the bra should fit snugly but not constrict your breathing. You want to be able to breathe naturally as the bra expands horizontally. The lower middle front of the bra should be flat across your skin—snug without pressure.
- Use the middle set of hooks when trying on the bra.
- The cup should not have wrinkles. If this is the case, try a smaller cup size. Sometimes different brands have slightly different size cups.
- If breast tissue comes out of the top of the cup or the side, try a larger size.
- The bra should not force your breasts to move in any direction, or cause them to rub together. A secure fitting cup should limit the motion.
- With the bra on, move your arms as you would do when moving the way you do during exercise. You shouldn't have any aggravation or restriction of the arm motion.
- The width is too wide if the band rides up in the back. Try lengthening the shoulder straps.
- Under the band, front and back, you should be able to insert one finger.
- Generally, you should be able to put two fingers under each strap.
- Try it on and move the way you do during exercise in front of the mirror to see if there is too much bounce.
- Walk/run for at least a short distance if the store staff will let you. Ensure that you have no irritation places, that breathing is comfortable, and that you can naturally move through the range of motion you will be doing during exercise.

Chaffing Issues

During warm weather, and on longer walks, most women have a few areas where clothing or body parts produce wear on other body parts. By reducing the friction in these areas, you'll reduce the irritation. The most common rubbed areas are between the legs, the lower front center area of the bra and just below and behind the shoulder, where the upper arm swings behind the body. You can significantly reduce both friction and aggravation by using vaseline and exercise products like "glide" that tend to last longer.

Many women who have chaffing problems apply the lubricant to both skin surfaces (and/or the garment) before the workout, and some carry a ziplock bag with the lubricant. As in most continuous rubbing situations, the sooner you reduce the friction, the less irritation. The "compression tights" (shorts made of lycra), have reduced chaffing between the legs dramatically. Sometimes, too much material and/or seaming in the shorts or top will increase chaffing. Minimal material is best.

Incontinence

The process of childbirth, aging and the reduction of estrogen often results in a natural weakening of support in the lower pelvis. It is fairly common that on longer workouts there may be some leakage of urine. Women who experience this can do the following:

- Do the kegel exercises: visit
  www.mayoclinic.com/health/kegel-exercises/WO00119
- Carefully reduce your intake of fluids 1-2 hours before exercise—and/or change liquids
- Wear dark shorts and bring a change of clothing for use after exercise
- Use an absorbant pad in the shorts
- Ask your doctor about a "bladder tack"

Loss of menstrual periods: amenorrhea

Years ago a leading researcher in female fertility reported that a steady increase in weekly mileage could cause a cessation of periods. Within a few hours he received calls from two of the leading female distance runners in the US. The first was concerned that the cessation would signify permanent loss of fertility, and he assured her that this was not indicated by the research. The second runner wanted to know if a certain amount of daily mileage would reduce fertility for that night (this was also not indicated).

There are many stresses in life that can cause the interruption of the woman's monthly cycle: poor diet, low level of body fat, too much exercise, and an accumulation of life stress. When the overall stress and the stress hormone cortisol reach a certain level in the individual, the hypothalamus in our brain reduces estrogen production and at some point menstrual periods cease or become irregular. Dr. Nicole Hagedorn, an OB/GYN herself, has noted that regular exercise, within your capabilities, can reduce stress in individuals.

But when women increase their weekly distance too quickly, the increase in cortisol, can be a primary cause of amenorrhea. We believe that too many miles per week kept us from conceiving for several years. It took five competitive marathons in 6 months to produce an injury, and the lack of exercise and one hormone shot during the recovery allowed for fertility to return. In other words, we owe our first child to an injury.

NANCY CLARK ON AMENORRHEA

The negative aspects of amenorrhea, as reported by Nancy Clark, are the following:

- loss of calcium from the bones
- an incidence of stress fractures 3 times greater than average (24% of athletes with no or irregular periods experience stress

fractures as compared to only 9% of regularly menstruating athletes)

- long-term problems with osteoporosis starting at an early age
- temporary loss of the ability to conceive a child

AMENORRHEA AND ANOREXIA

Although amenorrhea exists among women with no eating disorders, loss of menses is certainly symptomatic of restrictive, anorectic-type eating behaviors. The American Psychiatric Association's definition of anorexia lists „absence of at least three consecutive menstrual cycles" among the criteria. Other criteria include: weight loss 15% below normal for body type, intense fear of gaining weight or becoming fat and distorted body image (i.e., claiming to feel fat even when emaciated), all of which are concerns common to female athletes. If you feel as though you or someone you know are/is struggling to balance food and exercise, you might want to seek counseling from a trusted physician, dietitian and/or counselor. To find a local sports nutritionist, call 800-366-1655 or visit www.eatright.org and use the American Dietetic Association's referral network.

Note: Be sure to read "Overcoming an eating disorder" in the Heroes chapter

SUGGESTIONS FOR AMENORRHEA

- Cut quantity of exercise by 50% for several months. Swimming could be your exercise substitute. Even world class swimmers have a very low rate of amenorrhea.
- Increase your eating so that you will gain 5 pounds. This will not make you fat and often brings back the regularity of periods.
- Eat adequate protein and calories Amenorrheic athletes tend to eat less protein and calories than their regularly menstruating counterparts. Even if you are a vegetarian, remember that you still need adequate protein. Eat additional calories from yogurt, fish, beans, tofu and nuts.

- Eat at least 20% of your calories from fat. If you believe you will get fat if you eat fat, think again. Although excess calories from fat are easily fattening, some fat (20-30% of total calories; 40-60+ grams fat/day) is an appropriate part of a healthy sports diet. Nuts, peanut butter, salmon and olive oil are healthful choices.
- If your diet allows, include small portions of red meat 2 to 3 times per week. Surveys suggest runners with amenorrhea tend to eat less red meat and are more likely to follow a vegetarian diet than their regularly menstruating counterparts. Even in the general population, vegetarian women are five times more likely to have menstrual problems than meat eaters. It's unclear why meat seems to have a protective effect upon menses.
- Maintain a calcium-rich diet to help maintain bone density. A safe target is the equivalent of 3 to 4 servings per day of low-fat milk, yogurt and other calcium-rich foods. Being athletic, your bones benefit from the protective effect of exercise, but this does not compensate for lack of calcium nor lack of estrogen.
- Stay in touch with your OB-GYN. Many women runners have adjusted hormone supplementation, and returned to regular cycles.

Exercising through pregnancy

by Barbara Galloway

While I ran and walked through my pregnancies, I will never say that every woman should try this. Most can probably do light exercise for the first half to two-thirds of the term. Find a doctor who wants you to exercise, if possible. When that doctor tells you not to exercise (or cut the amount), you know that you should do so. Your doctor can be your "health coach" in the very best way.

Most women who are already exercising can continue for a while. Don't ever push through pain or any feeling that concerns you.

Stay cool. Exercise during the cool parts of the day. During the summer you can alternate walking with a swim or water running (or exercise in the air conditioned indoors).

Crunch Time—the final 3 months. During the last three months the baby's demand for oxygen increases significantly. This means that it will be very easy for you to become anaerobic during workouts that were easy a month before. If your doctor is still OK with your exercise, slow down and take "sit down breaks" between 3-5 minute segments.

It is very common during this last trimester to feel the Braxton-Hicks contractions when walking. Many doctors will tell you not to exercise when experiencing these. In my case, I was told that occasional contractions were normal and if they became stronger or more frequent, I should stop or switch exercises. I did not experience more serious contractions and continued to exercise until the day before delivery.

Exercising after pregnancy

After childbirth, many women find it difficult to exercise. First, you have to recover from your childbirth experience. Coping with hormonal changes and lactation will produce fatigue also.

When you start exercising after the birth of your child, assume that you are beginning all over again. Even veterans would benefit from following the beginning level program in this book, and adjust as needed. Start by walking gently for a few minutes every day. You will learn to treasure this time to yourself, or with a friend or two. The best exercise time of the day for me was right after nursing (or expressing milk). Walking, running, etc. is much more comfortable when you're not carrying the extra fluid and weight on your chest.

Dr. Diana Twiggs offers advice after running through several pregnancies.
- It's generally safe to continue the current program of exercise, but this is not a good time to start a new program. Gentle walking is usually OK, but check with your doctor.
- Heart rate limitations have fallen out of vogue.

- Keep your body temperature under control. This usually means less intensity, more hydration, and maybe indoor exercise (with air conditioning).
- Check with your doctor concerning your limit of core temperature increase.
- Running does NOT increase miscarriage rate.

Exercising while breastfeeding:
- Avoid dehydration and maintain proper nutrition to maintain milk supply.
- Long exercise sessions may slightly increase lactic acid for the next feed (not harmful but baby may not like the taste). You can always pump and dump right after if the baby doesn't like it.
- Wear a properly fitting running bra for comfort.

CHOOSING A STROLLER

There are a number of different models. Ask several women who use them for recommendations, and the cautions. The better models cost about $350 when new. Some running/walking clubs and running stores will try to match you up with women who are moving out of that phase of their life, and want to sell their stroller.

- The standard wheel size is about 20". Smaller wheels produce more bumps and don't handle uneven surface change very well.

- A safety leash is a necessity. Make sure that you have this in place and strapped securely around your arm/hand before you start. If you walk/run on hilly courses, a hand brake is desirable.

- Be sure that the surface and the size of the sidewalk is wide enough. BE SAFE!

Post-partum depression

Exercise after delivery can help women deal with the psychological challenges of childbirth. Post-partum depression is a serious condition and needs to be treated, often with medication. See a doctor!

PMS and menstrual issues

Let's face it, we women are hormonally challenged. If you are experiencing significant hormonal fluctuations, see a doctor who supports exercise.

Should I exercise during my period? Most women can, and many find that they do well when the period is taking place. We're aware of at least one woman who won an Olympic gold medal during hers. Planning ahead means carrying more tampons on your workouts, strategically charting a route with bathrooms, wearing dark shorts, etc. Dr. Nicole Hagedorn believes that long walks may be of great benefit during the week before the period, because it helps women sleep better.

Random aches, pains and cramping are common during ovulation, before and during menses. Unusual bleeding, severe pain etc. should be mentioned to your doctor.

Your energy level can be controlled by eating more often, combining nutrients, and moving around regularly. If you feel abnormally tired, talk to a dietitian. You may be anemic (this is common among women who have heavy periods). You should also have your hormone levels checked. Lack of sleep can be the result of low melatonin and high levels of cortisol. While unlikely, thyroid problems may be a cause.

Some of the medications that women take for PMS and menstrual issues can produce fatigue and sleepiness—and other side-effects. Check with your doctor or pharmacist for details.

Osteoporosis

After age 30, we lose bone mass each year. Weight bearing exercises, such as walking and running, have been shown to strengthen the bones (or at least maintain bone density) when there is adequate calcium in the diet. Some strength exercises, such as the ones noted in this book, can also strengthen connections to the spine, and can help to maintain bone strength in this very important structure. Ask strength experts for other exercises that can help you. Swimming and cycling are two examples of non-weight bearing exercises that will not promote bone density.

Technical explanation: According to Dr. John Bell, weight bearing activities create mechanical bend forces in our bones, altering the alignment of the hydroxyapatite crystals that form bone. This causes an electrical charge of piezo electricity that stimulates the osteocyte to lay down bone.

While a moderate amount of weight bearing exercise has been shown to stimulate bone density, doing too much (and/or dieting) can put exercisers into a caloric deficit. This stresses your body organism, significantly reducing estrogen production. The result is a loss of menstrual periods and reduction of bone density potential. Reference: „The Female Athlete Triad,“ Running & FitNews, American Running Association (ARA), June 1999. When you add the stress of pounding types of exercise (high impact aerobics, fast running, etc.) stress fracture risk increases rapidly according to our experience. You can reduce this risk by exercising longer one day and then reducing the amount the next day. It also helps on long walks/runs to insert liberal shuffle breaks (walk breaks) from the beginning.

Prevention: Exercise can help young women, in effect, put bone density "into storage". About 90% of female bone strength is established by the age of 18, and density peaks between age 25 and 30. Those who exercise strenuously and consume adequate calcium have a higher level of peak bone density. "Think of bone mass as a bank account that needs to be filled with the help of calcium and exercise to ensure strong bones later," says Catherine Niewochner, MD.

"Although calcium intake is often cited as the most important factor in healthy bones, our study suggests that exercise is really the predominant lifestyle determinant of bone strength in young women." Professor Tom Lloyd, Pennsylvania State College of

Medicine. (References: Journal of Applied Physiology Oct 2004, Journal of Pediatrics June 2004).

After the age of 30, bone density tends to decrease with each passing year. The object is to start with the highest level possible and then hold on to what you have. Weight bearing exercise (60 minutes every other day) and calcium intake (especially milk products and dark green vegetables) are two of the best activities to accomplish this. Most can also do a short walk, on the alternate day. The US National Institute of Health recommends that those above the age of 10 years old consume at least 1000 mg of calcium a day (about three 8 oz yogurts). At menopause, the recommendation rises to a minimum daily dose of 1500 mg (diet plus supplements). Vitamin D is crucial for calcium absorption: 400 IU is recommended for adults. As always, consult with your doctor about any individual issues or medical problems.

Bone loss behaviors

- Smoking: if you smoke, or are around secondhand smoke, try to quit and avoid a smoky environment

- Too much alcohol: no more than 2 glasses of wine or 2 beers per day

- Too much caffeine: limit to 3 cups of coffee per day, or equivalent

- Simple carbohydrate consumption: sugar, refined flour, sports drinks instead of milk. Limit simple carb consumption to no more than 20% of total carbohydrate consumption per day.

- Salt: if you need to add to the taste of food, add a little and avoid regular ingestion of salty foods

- Laxative use: try to limit to occasional use if needed.

- Restrictive and prolonged diets: diets don't tend to achieve long term fat loss anyway

- Cortisone drugs: consult with your doctor about drug issues

Menopause and after ...

All post-menopausal women should consider supplemental calcium and vitamin D (especially if sun exposure is limited) in order to prevent osteoporosis. There are a continuing series of questions about hormone replacement (estrogen). Read about the options and discuss with your doctor. While estrogen promotes calcium absorption, and a reduction of cardiovascular disease, it may increase risk of breast cancer, blood clots, and endometrial cancer.

Research shows that exercise continues to enhance bone density past the age of 50. Studies of middle aged and post menopausal women have found that at least every other day exercise, adding up to more than 7 miles total a week, resulted in increased bone density in the trunk. Walking and running also produced a density increase in the femoral neck bones.

Bone density tests can usually tell you whether you're at risk for osteoporosis. Dr Richard S. Newman, from the American Medical Athletic Association and ARA website, recommends that those possibly at risk for osteoporosis should talk to their doctors about a „DEXA scan". This sonogram technology calculates bone density in a 15-minute session, fully clothed on an exam table. There are other tests, including a CT scan test. Osteoporosis is indicated when your bone density reading shows that you are a certain percentage below peak density, based upon age.

Exercise, calcium and vitamin D supplementation and medication can help you hold the bone density you have. There are also some drugs that have been very effective in this area (Fosamax for example). Again, talk to your doctor.

Dr. Ruth Parker recommends the following website links:

http://www.nih.gov/news/WordonHealth/dec2003/osteo.htm
http://www.mayoclinic.com/health/exercise/HQ01676
http://www.cdc.gov/powerfulbones/
http://www.mayoclinic.com/health/exercise/SM00059
http://consensus.nih.gov/2000/2000Osteoporosis111html.htm

Menopause

Most exercising women who are going through menopause tell me that they feel better and have a better attitude on the walking/running days. Exercise helps women sleep better, combating the insomnia that is common.

The symptoms and intensity of menopause differ greatly. Your greatest asset is a doctor who understands the benefits/effects of exercise and wants you to do it. After you talk through most of the symptoms and make some minor adjustments, you will find what works for you. But whenever you have a possible medical issue, run it by your doctor.

Your energy level can be controlled by eating more often, combining nutrients, and moving around regularly. If you feel abnormally tired, talk to a dietician. Thyroid problems are common as we age, and significant loss of energy can be a symptom. If you've tried to deal with your energy loss through nutrition, etc., without success, ask your doctor about possible thyroid issues. You should have your hormone levels checked. Lack of sleep can be the result of low melatonin and high levels of cortisol.

Hormone supplementation is a very complex issue and should be discussed with your doctor. Because of the reduction of estrogen production, during and after menopause, and sleeplessness due to low melatonin, many women respond well to supplements. OB/GYN Nicole Hagedorn believes that when supplementation is advised, that "bioidentical hormones" work better for most women. These have the same molecular structure as the ones produced by your body. As with all important medical issues, check with your doctor.

Our friend Nancy Clark has the following information concerning the issue of weight gain during menopause.

Women, Weight & Menopause

by Nancy Clark

"No matter what I do, I can't seem to stop gaining weight..." Frustrated with her expanding waist, this former athlete, like others who are approaching menopause, is frightened about run-away weight gain. She started dieting and exercising harder to counter the flab and, over the din of the exercycle, asked, "Are women *doomed* to gain weight midlife?" Here are the answers to some questions middle-aged women (and their husbands, children and family members) commonly ask about weight and menopause.

Question: Do women inevitably gain fat with menopause?
No! Women do not always gain weight with menopause. Yes, women commonly get fatter and thicker around the middle as the fat settles in and around the abdominal area. But the changes are due more to lack of exercise and a surplus of calories than to a reduction of hormones. Young athletes with amennorhea (and reduced hormones) do not get fat...

In a three-year study with more than 3,000 women (initial age 42 to 52 years), the average weight gain was 4.6 pounds. The weight gain occurred in all women, regardless of their menopause status. (Sternfeld, Am J Epidemiol, 2004).

Question: If weight gain is not due to the hormonal shifts of menopause, what does cause it? Here are a few culprits:

- Menopause occurs during a time of life when women may become less active. That is, if your children have grown up and left home, you may find yourself sitting more in front of a TV or computer screen, rather than running up and down stairs, carrying endless loads of laundry.

- A less active lifestyle not only reduces your calorie needs, but also results in a decline in muscle mass. Because muscle drives your metabolic rate, less muscle means a slower metabolism and fewer calories burned. (That is, of course, unless you wisely preserve your muscle by exercising)

- Sleep patterns commonly change in midlife. Add on top of that sleep-disrupting night sweats and a husband who snores, and many women end up feeling exhausted most of the time. Exhaustion and sleep deprivation can easily drain motivation to routinely exercise.

- Sleep deprivation is associated with weight gain. Adults who sleep less than seven hours per night tend to be heavier than their well-slept counterparts. When you are sleep deprived, your appetite grows. That is, the hormone that curbs your appetite (leptin) is reduced and the hormone that increases your appetite (grehlin) become more active. (Taheri, PLoS Med, 2004) Hence, you can have a hard time differentiating between "Am I tired?" or "Am I hungry?" You hear the cookie monster answer "You're hungry and need many cookies...!"

- Menopause coincides with career success, including business meals at nice restaurants, extra wine, plush vacations and cruises. Read that more calories and less exercise.

- By midlife, most women are tired of dieting and depriving themselves of tempting foods; they may have been dieting since puberty! The "No, thank you" that prevailed at previous birthday parties now becomes "Yes, please."

Tips for preventing midlife weight gain and optimizing health:

The best way to prevent weight gain is to exercise and maintain an active lifestyle. Research suggests women who exercise do not the gain the weight and waist of their non-exercising peers (Sternfeld, Am J Epidem 2004). The exercise program should include both aerobic exercise (to enhance cardiovascular health) and strengthening exercise (to preserve muscle strength and bone density). The book „Strong Women Stay Thin" by Miriam Nelson is a good resource for developing a health-protective exercise program.

- Despite popular belief, taking hormones to counter the symptoms of menopause does not contribute to weight gain. If anything, hormone replacement therapy may help curb midlife weight gain. (DiCarlo, Menopause, 2004)

- Menopausal women need a strong calcium intake: 1,200 to 1,500 mg calcium/day, or the equivalent of a serving of milk or yogurt at each meal. If you are tempted to take a supplement instead of consume low-fat dairy foods, think again. One supplement does not replace the whole package of health-protective nutrients in low-fat milk and yogurt. Also, recent research suggests women who drink 3 or more servings of milk or yogurt per day tend to be leaner than milk-abstainers. Milk can help you lose—not gain—weight.

- If you have gained undesired fat, do not diet. If you have been dieting for 35 to 40 years of your adult life, you should have learned by now that dieting does not work. Rather, you need to learn how to eat healthfully. This means, fuel your body with enough breakfast, lunch and afternoon snack to curb your appetite (and energize your exercise program). Then, eat a lighter dinner. *Think small calorie deficit.* That is, consuming 100 fewer calories after dinner (theoretically) translates into losing 10 pounds of fat per year.

- To find peace with food and your body, meet with a registered dietitian (RD) who specializes in sports nutrition. This professional can develop a personalized food plan that fits your needs. To find a local RD, go to www.eatright.org and enter your zip code into the referral network.

Also ask yourself: Am I really overweight? Maybe there is just more of you to love. Your body may not be quite as perfect as it once was at the height of your athletic career, but it can be good enough. I encourage you to focus on being fit and healthy, rather than being thin at any cost. No weight will ever do the enormous job of creating midlife happiness.

Sports Nutritionist Nancy Clark, MS, RD counsels sports-active people at her private practice in the Healthworks Fitness Center (617-383-6100) in Chestnut Hill, MA. Her best-selling Nancy Clark's Sports Nutrition Guidebook, Third Edition *offers additional weight-management help, as do her* Food Guide for Marathoners: Tips for Everyday Champions *and* The Cyclist's Food Guide: Fueling for the Distance. *All are available via www.nancyclarkrd.com.*

Links:

National Diabetes Education Program (NDEP)
Internet: *www.ndep.nih.gov*
National Diabetes Information Clearinghouse (NDIC)
Internet: *www.diabetes.niddk.nih.gov*
Weight-control Information Network (WIN)
Internet: *win.niddk.nih.gov/notes/index.htm*
National Heart, Lung, and Blood Institute (NHLBI) Information Center
Internet: *www.nhlbi.nih.gov*
Centers for Disease Control and Prevention (CDC)
Internet: *www.cdc.gov/diabetes*

Heroes:
Women Like You Who Burned It Off

85 pounds lighter and counting

Tracy B added the usual weight during her pregnancy, and kept on adding. When the scales told her that she was almost 100 pounds over her "healthy" weight, she walked out the door and kept going. A local charity marathon team provided her with a cause and good friends, as she walked her way to the marathon. "The marathon team became a part of me—like a little extension of my family". Instead of trying a restrictive diet, she simply tried reasonably sized meals and no high fat snacks. She's still 10 pounds from her goal, but is still losing. Be sure to see Tracy's tips in the "Fabulously Full Figured" chapter.

98 pounds off...and still losing

Karen had been overweight most of her life, and, as she puts it "definitely not athletic". But she had taken the path used by women through the ages: "I had tried every diet, spent an embarrassing amount of money on diet programs." The weight would drop for a few weeks or months and then, steadily rise until it surpassed the pre-diet amount. For some reason, surpassing 200, 225 and 250 pounds was OK. When the nurse told her she weighed 271, she held it in until reaching her car and then the tears flowed.

When her friend Jo decided to train for the Country Music Half Marathon (Nashville) Karen was determined to use this race as a goal to be an every-other-day walker. Her fitness improved week by week, she found the challenge of this 13 miler highly motivating. The run-walk-run method allowed her to move from a walker to a runner. So, in her late 30's, weighing 230 pounds Karen ran a minute and walked a minute. Sedentary spouse Paul was so impressed by her steady progress that he began running also, at 278 pounds. Two years later, Paul had lost 90 pounds. Karen has lost 98 pounds, and is still losing. As Karen approached the finish line of the Country Music 13.1 miler, the tears started flowing again—for all of the right reasons. Karen and Paul schedule vacations around running events now, and get stressed when they cannot run.

"If you're a beginner, start with short run - walk intervals. It's better to set realistic goals that you can meet and then adjust them as you improve." Karen

145 LBS LIGHTER

I truly believe running has allowed me to cope with the mental and physical stresses of daily life, motherhood, and work more effectively."

Angela was an overweight kid from an obese family. By the age of 35, she weighed 280 pounds with high blood pressure, and back, knee, and hip pain. She also had a serious gastric reflux problem, and surgery was recommended.

In January of 2005, after months of psychological counseling and exercise (primarily walking and elliptical) she had the gastric bypass operation. She soon discovered that surgery doesn't change a genetic predisposition to obesity, nor the desire to cope with stress by overeating (many patients gain back some of their weight after these surgeries). Because of her surgery, she had to eat less and avoid certain foods because of their physical side effects.

Having enjoyed the stress relief of the pre-operation exercise, Angela continued to walk. Six months later, and 85 pounds lighter, she decided to "step it up" by inserting some short running segments into her walks, and completed a 10K, and then a half marathon during the training season. By this time she had lost a total of 120 pounds, crediting running with "revving up" the fat burning.

Looking for some guidance, she joined our Galloway Training program, finished the Richmond Marathon and set her sights on the "original" marathon in Athens, Greece. Despite some health setbacks during the training, she kept improving endurance and lost another 25 pounds. On the difficult Greek course (with a 13 mile hill) Angela set a new personal record by 22 minutes!

"To lose it and keep it off it has to be a lifestyle change, whether it is 30 pounds or 100 pounds - It also has to come from your heart that you want to do it."

Even when Kathryn was severely obese and had trouble jogging a few steps, she had a vision that she could become a marathoner. At first, it took her 25 minutes to cover a mile. At this pace, she would not be allowed to continue in the race, because the course would have been closed—and she had 25 more miles to go! While many would have given up, Kathryn got moving. At first, she set her sights on one mile at a time and one pound at a time—then, one week at a time.

In spite of the fatigue she experienced during marathon training, Kathryn discovered an infusion of motivation from inside. Here are some of her tips.

Before   After

Kathryn Lost Over 100 Pounds: Portion Control and Marathon Training

- A short term goal seems easier to reach.

- Once you reach that goal immediately set another one.

- Advising others to train for a goal was so motivating—helping others while helping myself.

- When you are coming toward the finish line, look at it as a start—improving the rest of your life.

- I didn't want to cut out foods that I liked – So I ate them, but I cut the portion.

- Food in gives fuel for walking/running.

- Walking and running burned off the fat—a little bit each week.

"What kept me going? I knew how good I was feeling inside, what I was doing for my health. I felt stronger. If your goal is to finish a marathon, then do it, but don't stop!"

Sherry began her journey at 348 pounds—and has lost more than 150 lbs (see her tips in next chapter)

A normal 25 year old female should be happy, healthy and full of life. At 25 I was lazy, super obese, unhealthy, depressed, and had minimal self-confidence. I always had a weight problem: 40 pounds overweight at 15, 70 pounds at 18. By the time I graduated college and married at age 22, I was an incredible 125 pounds overweight, and at my twenty-fifth birthday, I weighed 348 pounds!

"I cannot pinpoint one reason that led me to being super obese with a BMI of 56. I did not have an easy time growing up. My older sister was gravely ill when I was young, and my mom had a difficult time dealing with depression and anxiety. At times I felt like I was not loved, which led to sexual abuse as a teenager. I was diagnosed with Polycystic Ovarian Syndrome (PCOS), which results in fertility problems and heightened levels of insulin resistance. I loved to eat carbs, which really packed on the pounds. It was an atrocious cycle—the more I would eat, the less I could exercise. The heavier I got, the more I became depressed, which led me to eating more to comfort myself."

"My Breaking Point My husband and I tried to start a family for months, with no success. Hormone therapy didn't work either and triggered hair loss in clumps, mood swings and hot flashes. I was miserable. Finally, we were scheduled to see a reproductive endocrinologist but were then rejected because I was too heavy and the pregnancy risks to me and the baby would be too great. I knew that I was on track for a heart attack and I loved my husband too much to leave him tragically at a young age."

"My Decision to change my life started with a gastric bypass operation. I lost weight quickly and easily because my stomach was now the size of an egg. My new stomach was a tool, and being successful at weight loss would be a lifelong commitment. As soon as I was released from the hospital I began an exercise regimen, mall walking and a ladies-only gym. The exercise was helping to keep the fat off. Then, My friend Susan won an entry in the Peachtree Road Race, the world's largest 10k. I thought anyone who could run a 5k was an elite athlete! I was in awe when she finished the race in 80 minutes. Then came the great visualization: If she could do it, then so can I!

"Ready, Set, Go! There was no starting gun to signal the start of my training, but I sure was fired up. I set a goal of running in the Kaiser Permanente Corporate 5k, just over a month away. The night before the race I woke up in horrible pain at 2 AM. My husband rushed me to the ER where they discovered I had a hole somewhere in my digestive system. I had emergency surgery, which led to a fourteen inch scar, 40 staples, and a week's vacation at Gwinnett Medical Center. I was distraught. I felt that everything I worked hard to achieve was ruined. I cried for three hours straight. The nurses tried to make me feel better, but I was inconsolable. At this point, my only dream was shattered."

"A week after being released from the hospital, I started walking, even with pain. I signed up for a local 10k trained and finished— I was a runner! I immediately found my husband and announced I wanted to run a marathon. He pretty much thought I was insane, but I joined a training group, dealt with the gastric/fluid absorption problems, excessive loose skin and back pain. I crossed the Chicago Marathon finish line and a wave of emotions overcame me. At 348 pounds, I never once imagined being able to run to my mailbox. Through many trials and tribulation, and mostly hard work, I was able to lose the weight and do what I once thought was unthinkable."

"Through sweat, hard work, and even a few tears I was able to accomplish each of the goals I set for myself because I developed a strong mental attitude, and took charge over my health and fitness. I had the seeds of these capabilities when I was a depressed 348 pounder—and didn't know it. You do too.

Note: Sherry recently finished one of the most arduous sporting events—Ironman Florida—and beat her expected time by hours!" Be sure to see her tips in the "Fabulously Full Figured" chapter which follows.

Overcoming an Eating Disorder

Julie was an overweight child, rode horses, ate pop tarts and tater tots, and had a wonderful Mom, but experienced self-esteem issues. As a 9th grader (180 pounds, 5' 10") she broke her foot falling off a horse, hobbled around and got depressed, and reduced her quantity of food. As she lost weight, she received positive feedback from peers for the first time in her life ("You look good"), and started to feel good about herself. So she ate even less and lost more—down to 110 lbs!

"I don't remember when, or how, but I noticed things starting to change. I was still getting attention, but it was from those with concern. I started riding again and my trainer approached me and asked me to feel free to come to her if I had a problem because she had been there before. I started feeling light-headed all the time, I would try to stand up and literally fall right back down. I quit getting my period and it was a struggle to walk, let alone ride. Bottom line was that I felt weak, and I knew I needed to do something about it."

She started running, and walking (alternating mailboxes) but was so hungry and weak that she ate more, became energetic and felt strong, settling into a healthy weight of 145 lbs. Then came college. Caring for horses, studying hard, commuting to school took time and she stopped running. "My mind went into a hard downward spiral of self-esteem once again, and I started something new, turning to food for comfort. I didn't do drugs or smoke, but I turned to food for that quick endorphin boost. I would find myself tired, frustrated, and disgusted, and would lock myself in my room literally gorging on whatever was in sight." The scales exceeded the 200 mark, she hated herself, and hid from friends.

"I wrote in a diary every night about how I would change, only to fail the following day. Again, I had hit a very low point and knew I needed to do something. Knowing I could not control my eating habits, I started trying to control something I knew I could, my exercise. I started running again. And again, experienced the same psychological response as I did in high school. I felt better about myself, I started to lose weight, and I was able to pull myself out of the slump."

Julie was inspired: to read about proper nutrition, to eat more meals each day, and to train for a marathon. "My mood sailed and I could conquer the world, or could I? I trained (running straight out) to the point of completing my first half marathon, which sent me to straight burn out. My runs became a constant struggle, and I started to hate every second of them. I stopped running, and up went the weight, down went the self-esteem and mood."

Julie fell in love, with Chris, and they decided to train for a marathon. "I stumbled across the most wonderful concept, something that up until now my body had known but I did not, eating gave you fuel."

She started running stronger and faster and broke all of her personal records.
"I no longer run because I eat too much, I eat so that I can run. I have dropped weight, but my body composition has completely changed. My body fat is the lowest it has ever been, and guess what, I'm eating Reese's Peanut Butter Cups and white bread! Who would have thought!" Julie S.

Fabulously Full Figured?

While we were writing this book, a growing number of women who are larger than the average citizen, asked for a chapter dealing with some special issues. After consulting with a variety of those who have fought these battles, and are still doing so successfully, the following information is offered—with inspirational stories. Some of the stories involve women who started using walking as exercise, but got into running. You can choose the type of exercise you wish—don't give up!

85 pounds lighter and counting

Tracy B added the usual weight during her pregnancy, and kept on going. When the scales told her that she was almost 100 pounds over her "healthy" weight, she walked out the door and kept going. A local charity marathon team provided her with a cause and good friends, as she walked her way to the marathon. "The marathon team I became a part of is like a little extension of my family". Instead of trying a restrictive diet, she simply tried reasonable size meals and no high fat snacks. She's still 10 pounds from her goal, but is still losing.

"Don't look at the big number of pounds you need to lose. Set an attainable goal, maybe 10 pounds at a time. And if you fall off the wagon, get back on and don't beat yourself up about it. Be proud of how hard you are working"

Tips from Tracy

1. "Never give up on yourself and be very proud of yourself for any effort you're making to make yourself healthier and fit.

2. Don't beat yourself up for „falling off the wagon" - this will happen at some point. Just dust yourself off and make that day your „first day" again - don't look back!

3. Don't let friends or family members discourage your efforts. I know this sounds odd because these people should be your support system - but some people don't adapt to change very well and can feel threatened by the new you and your new group of friends.

4. Eat a very healthy, well-balanced diet. If you're not sure how to get started with this either consult this book or check with your doctor or nutritionist.

5. Then make yourself a fat burning machine. When I first started walking I would walk on my breaks at work, my lunch hour and then do my regular distance when I got home.

6. Be sure to cross-train. Not only is this good for your muscles, but it's good for your brain too.
   You deserve your time to exercise!

7. I think the biggest thing for women (no matter what size) is that you deserve to give this to yourself. My job and my family get me for 14 out of the 16 hours I put in a day. I allow myself to take those other 2 hours for me - guilt free! I need this - distance walking defines who I am. In return, my family gets a healthier and happier Mom! I want to be around to see my kids grow up and then run circles around my grandkids!"

Sherry's Tips
—more than 150 pounds lost ... runs marathons

Exercise was the theme in rising out of depression and into a vigorous life. Be sure to read her moving and inspirational story in the "Heroes" chapter. Here are her points.

- "If you are considerably overweight/obese, see your doctor, and get shoes from a good running store.

- Winded when doing even gentle exercise? Then walk slowly at first.

- Excess skin—use girdles, spandex, knee-to-chest Flexee, to keep it from getting in the way.

- Back issues: physical therapy can help. Ab strengthening helped a bit. The only thing that ultimately helped me was getting my excess skin removed after weight loss. Don't lean over or look down—stay upright!

- Make sure to shower and dry off properly. Excess skin and moisture is a prime habitat for a yeast infection.

- Larger women feel self-conscious when exercising. Ladies-only full-service gyms are a good supportive environment to get started. I found that my fellow runners are really nice people-no matter how much faster they are than you. As heavy as I was, I always got friendly waves and greetings on the running trails. Be proud, don't look down!

- Don't be afraid of your first race. Most races have a big walking group. Sign up with friends"....Sherry

Bras
Be prepared to pay significantly more than you would pay for your everyday bra—sometimes as much as you would pay

for your shoes. Remember that bras usually last a lot longer than shoes.

There are a growing number of bras designed for specific types of exercise, based upon cup size. Many large breasted women have reported success with the Enell brand and the Fiona model from Moving Comfort. Champion has a seamless underbra with underwire that has also been successful.

- Many of the well constructed "workout bras" are not supportive for runners. The elastic in these products (for twisting and extraneous motion in tennis, pilates, etc.) allows for significant bouncing and stress when running.

- Comfort: Look first at the fibers next to your skin. The microfibers can move moisture away from your skin, reducing chaffing (see next section), moisture chill, and weight increase due to the absorption of sweat by cotton and similar fibers.

C, D & E Cups: More support is needed. Look for a bra that will fit each breast, and a strap that has minimal or no elastic. The best placement of the straps will differ among individuals—so try on a variety of bras to find the configuration that matches up with your body. If you receive pressure on the shoulders, where the straps press down, padded straps can help. See the "woman's issues" chapter of this book for more on bra fitting.

Exercise improves health and well-being—even when obese. This is the finding of numerous studies at the Cooper Research Institute (Dallas, Texas) and other institutions. At Cooper, the obese-but-fit subjects were shown to have a healthier profile than sedentary thin subjects.

Worried about the way they look in public, many heavier women don't exercise. That's too bad because it is clear that even 10 minutes of regular movement of the feet will bestow a better attitude, and can lead to higher self esteem. Short exercise segments will also burn fat! It is easier to piece together several segments of 100-200 steps than 30 minutes at one time. Smaller segments tend to reduce appetite increase in most of the exercisers that we've heard from on the issue.

Read the Fat Burning section of this book. The "set point" mechanism can help you understand fat deposition, and what you can do to hold your own—or lower it. And please, don't go on a restrictive diet. These usually produce water loss, and increased fat accumulation and more weight, after the diet has ended.

The low-carbohydrate scam

There is no doubt that low-carb diets can help you lose weight....water weight. Such a loss is superficial and easily gained back. Here's how it works. To perform physical exertion, you need a quick energy source called glycogen, which is a form of processed carbohydrate, that is stored in the muscles, liver and other areas. It must be replenished every day. The storage areas for glycogen are limited and glycogen is also the primary source for vital organs like the brain. A good quantity of water (needed in the use of glycogen) is stored near the glycogen storage areas.

By starving themselves of carbohydrates, low-carb dieters experience a severe reduction in glycogen—and energy level. But if the glycogen isn't there, water is not stored either. The elimination of these two substances can result in significant weight loss within days—continuing for a few weeks.

Fat is not being burned off. In fact, fat is often a significant ingredient in many of the low-carb diets. As low-carb dieters eat more fat, they often increase the fat on the body. But they don't realize this because the scales are showing a total loss—due to the water/glycogen reduction. When they replace water and glycogen later, the weight goes back on. Soon the overall body weight is greater than before because of the added fat from the low-carb diet.

Because the glycogen energy source is low or depleted, low-carbers will not have much energy for exercise. This is why you will hear folks on this diet complain of low energy, lack of desire to exercise, inability to finish a workout, and sometimes lack of mental focus (low glycogen means less fuel for the brain).

Even if you "tough it out" or cheat on the diet a little, your capacity to do even moderately strenuous exertions will be greatly reduced. With your energy stores near empty, exercising becomes a real struggle, and no fun. The reduction in exercise and movement in general usually results in a lower metabolism rate—meaning that you won't be burning many calories as you go about your life activities.

LOW-CARB DIETS DON'T TELL YOU THIS….

- You don't burn fat—many gain fat
- The weight loss is usually water loss, with glycogen loss
- Almost everyone on this diet resumes regular eating, within a few weeks or months
- Almost all low-carb dieters gain back more weight than they lost.
- You lose the energy and motivation to exercise
- You lose exercise capacity that can help to keep the weight off when you resume eating normally.
- Your metabolism rate goes down—making it harder to keep the weight off

Group support is huge—Join or start a charity fund raising or training group, such as that for *www.BreastCancerMarathon.com*. The programs at Weight Watchers and Curves can be very successful because of group support. For Galloway Training Groups, visit *www.JeffGalloway.com*

Family and Friend Issues

By Barbara Galloway

Support is crucial! Let's face facts, women tend to look for support from family members and other women, when facing a challenge in life. When your close friends and family members are behind you as you get into exercise, the problems don't seem as difficult. Without support, there will more stress in scheduling and completing your workouts. Simply telling your friends and family that this is important to you will help in most cases. When you recruit your spouse, child, sister and friends, to join you as you walk (even if the kids ride their bikes) you'll feel a sense of teamwork. Kids and husbands are aware of the positive changes in you (on your exercise days) and are usually not bashful about telling you: "You're not as grumpy after your workout—please exercise today."

Choosing your exercise companion or group

You'll be more motivated to exercise if your group (or running companion) is waiting for you. Some women call their friends in other cities during a walk, and talk as if they are going along the trail together. The bonding during a workout often produces lifelong friendships. Secrets shared on a stress relieving walk/run usually need to stay there. There are many training programs that offer a variety of pace groups. Some are listed on my website: www.JeffGalloway.com. Be sure to choose a group that allows you to exercise comfortably, so that you don't have to extend your stride to keep up.

Helping people in need—including yourself

Linda Gibson articulates well the effectiveness of raising funds for a good cause—which helped her get "hooked" on the fitness lifestyle. "Middle-aged women tend to put everyone else first. This is why I chose to participate in a charity event. This way, I was doing something for others but, in reality, I was really doing it for myself. The fact that I had a trainer and started with the appropriate gear was very important to my success. I would have dropped out had it not been for the support my coach and teammates gave me all the time."

Goal: Train for an event

The best example I've seen of a charity event (with training program) is The NATIONAL MARATHON TO FIGHT BREAST CANCER (www.breastcancermarathon.com). All of the race entry fees (100%) go to breast cancer research at the Mayo Clinic and care for underserved women. There are various fundraising possibilities for men and women, including the chance to earn a trip to the event weekend in Jacksonville Beach, FL for an upbeat weekend. When you finish a marathon or half marathon, you experience a series of rewards.

When your significant other doesn't exercise

Honesty is the best policy. Tell your spouse (partner) that your exercise is very important to you, and that you need support. Explain the positive changes you've experienced. Extend the offer to exercise together.

Getting Kids or Adults Into Exercise

Mothers who exercise are powerful role models to their children. Leading by example, and then encouraging children to enjoy exercise is a gift that keeps on giving. Kids learn that an exercise session can increase energy, improve attitude, increase motivation, release stress, and positively impact schoolwork. Studies (listed in Jeff's book FIT KIDS—SMARTER KIDS) show that kids who get into regular exercise tend to do better academically, and in life. When you help people improve the quality of their lives you'll not only help them: studies show that this tends to boost *your* immune system.

- Your motivation to exercise increases when you serve as a role model. You'll also inspire yourself to learn more about fitness. Most adults who teach kids find that they study and learn the principles of training better as they explain them to others.

- Get them a good textbook—and a journal—My book Women's Complete Guide to Walking, for example.

- Start with a little exercise, and gradually increase. Children will often do a lot more than they should at first, and then get sore and discouraged. Hold them back and they can be successful in every workout!

- Make each session enjoyable—especially during the first month. If your coachee is huffing and puffing, slow the pace, walk more slowly, and make other adjustments from the beginning of every exercise session. If there is any sign of struggle, then stop for that day. Never push through pain.

Low Blood Sugar

Before starting, if you suspect that your friend or child is experiencing low blood sugar, have pieces of an energy bar and water, etc. about 30-45 minutes before the start. Have a reward after each session—especially a snack to reload that is composed of 80% carbohydrate and 20% protein. On some special occasions, however, it's OK to have a reward snack that may be a little more decadent than usual—if it keeps them motivated.

Find interesting areas where you can walk or exercise— scenic areas, smooth trails, fun health clubs

Convenient routes near school or home, will lead to more exercise sessions a year. But once a week or so, an excursion to an interesting area can be very rewarding. It's great to have variety, and you should give your coachee some choice.

On each exercise session, have a joke, a juicy story or a controversial issue

This will break the ice, inject some humor, and result in a positive bonding experience. With beginners (adults or kids) who are struggling with motivation, the humorous moments provide a series of positive reinforcements.

Don't push too hard, but encourage, and reinforce a good attitude

One of the most difficult decisions in coaching is whether to push or back off—whether to use a pat on the back or a kick on the butt. In general, it is important that the person exercise regularly. When motivation is down, reduce the intensity to reduce discomfort. The ultimate success is realized when the new exerciser wants to do it.

Rewards work!

After a certain number of weeks, or after reaching a certain level of fitness, surprise the coachee with a reward. It doesn't have to be something expensive or exotic. The reward allows the new exerciser to focus on his or her progress, and feel the satisfaction that comes from steady exercise.

When your coachee is ready, find a fun event to attend

Races are such positive experiences for new walkers or runners. Teachers can set up "success days" when beginners can become athletes. Participation and completion is the goal of these events—not winning. Just having a race date on a calendar will provide the beginner with the identity of an athlete that will increase motivation.

Tell him or her about your mistakes

When you open up to your new exerciser with a personal story from you, the lessons become more powerful.

Don't over-sell exercise

The benefits are so powerful that almost everyone who stays with it for 6 months, will continue. Exercising with the new athlete on the tough days, and congratulating her for the dedication are powerful reinforcers. But if your coachee is falling asleep during your one hour speech on the benefits, you know that you've stepped over the line.

Your greatest reward will be an independent, fit person
Take it as a real compliment that your coachee will need less and less of your guidance. This means that you were an excellent coach, and that he or she can find another person to coach, thereby enriching another life.

Kids Programs:
A growing number of fitness programs for children can be licensed or franchised in local areas. Here are some of them.

Girls On The Run This fitness program is designed to help build genuine self esteem based upon accomplishment through running and walking and life lessons. "We measure success with the overall manner in which the girls respect themselves and others....how they feel in their own skin".
www.girlsontherun.org

Marathon Kids® is a ten year old non-profit, program conducted through schools for K-5th grade children. Over 100,000 kids participate in various cities around the US.
www.MarathonKids.com

Crim Festival of Races, Flint MI Youth Fun and Fitness Program involves over 10,000 kids from 38 schools and youth clubs. It is a model grass-roots kids fitness program tied in with an event.

Stretch-n-Grow is a comprehensive fitness program for kids committed to helping educators and parents establish a foundation of exercise, proper nutrition and a healthy lifestyle. Info@stretchandgrow.com

Kidsrunning.com has several books with great program suggestions: Happy Feet, Healthy Food, Your Child's First Journal of Exercise and Healthy Eating, The Treasure of Health and Happiness.

JUST RUN Monterey County is a FREE program funded by the Big Sur International Marathon and private donations. The goal is to promote fitness and healthy lifestyles in grades 2-8. www.justrun.org

Websites:
Information
www.Kidsrunning.com
www.fitnessforyouth.umich.edu
www.fitnessmba.com
www.kidzworld.com
www.acefitness.org/ofk/youthfitness
www.cdc.gov/verb
www.KidsHealth.org
www.fitnessfinders.net

Games and activities
www.kidsrunning.com
www.pecentral.com
www.runnersworld.com

Eating with a Purpose

Understanding Fat Accumulation & Burn-off
Your Fat Burning Tool Kit (BMI, websites, step counter, etc.)
Managing The Calorie Budget
The Eating Plan: Meal by Meal
Practical Eating Issues
Good Blood Sugar Level = Motivation

plus: Nutrition Advice from Nancy Clark

Understanding Fat Accumulation & Burn-off

Fat is our genetic insurance policy against disaster—and much more. It is the efficient fuel your body can use while exercising. A biological mechanism called the "set point" ensures that we have an increase in fat accumulation, with each year of age, to increase the chance of survival in case of prolonged sickness, starvation, or injury. So it's natural to weigh more at 47 than you did at 40. Adding more fat with age is what we are supposed to do, and not necessarily a sign of "letting yourself go". But there is hope for those who want to lose some of this "insurance". By learning how to budget calories you can enjoy foods as you gain control over your fat accumulation. Reducing food intake by itself is not the fun part of lowering fat levels—nor is it a successful strategy over the long term. While going on a "diet" (reducing the amount of food consumed) can definitely result in a body weight reduction, this is almost always a temporary situation. Food deprivation activates what we call the "starvation reflex" that activates a "rebound" in fat accumulation once the diet is over. Exercise has been shown to be the best way to burn fat and keep it off. By increasing gentle exercise as you control consumption you set up a successful process that you can control. Best part is that with exercise, you don't have to be hungry all the time.

Exercise brings joy to your life. If you haven't experienced this, you haven't been doing it right. In the exercise section you'll find a fat reduction training schedule that is gentle, has a number of options, and burns fat without pain. When exercise is right for you, a positive attitude and a glow is bestowed by every session—you want to come back and do it again. Exercise gives you more energy for your day, and erases or controls stress buildup while it revs up the furnace that can burn off the potential energy in storage.

With this plan you are eating often, regularly moving yourself, and becoming an active person involved in life. This gives you the energy to think clearly, perform your daily activities, and enjoy family and life. You're in control.

How does fat accumulate?

When you eat a food that has fat in it, you might as well put the fat grams into a syringe and inject it into your stomach or thigh. A gram of fat eaten is a gram of fat deposited into the fat storage areas on your body. In addition, when you eat more calories than you need that day, from protein (fish, chicken, beef, tofu) and carbohydrate (breads, fruits, vegetables, sugar), the excess is converted into fat and stored.

The Set Point ensured survival of the species

For more than a million years of human evolution the human body has been programmed to hold on to the fat you have stored because of a powerful principle: survival of the species. Before humans understood disease and food storage, our ancestors were susceptible to sweeping infections and starvation. Those who had above average fat stores survived periods of starvation and sickness, and passed on the fat accumulation adaptation to their children. The replication of this process over thousands of generations has resulted in the powerful *set point*.

This biologically engineered survival mechanism is programmed to increase the fat storage levels each year. Changing the set point puts you into a confrontation with a process that has been in place for over a million years, making you the underdog. It is possible to reduce fat levels but you must set realistic goals for fat management.

The lowest set point is experienced in the early 20's

Many experts agree that by about the age of 25 we have accumulated a level of fat that the body intuitively marks as its lowest level. This set point is programmed to increase a little each year. The amount of increase is so small in the 20's and early 30s, that we usually don't realize that we're adding it—until about 10 years later, when it's time to go to a class reunion, etc.

Humans are supposed to carry around fat. But your set point does too good a job, continuing to add to the percentage, each year, every year. And the amount of increase seems to be significantly greater as we get older. Even when you've had a year when stress or illness prevented the usual increase, the set point makes up by increasing appetite more than normal during the following year or two. Go ahead, shout "Unfair!" as loud as you wish. Your set point doesn't argue, it just makes another deposit. There is hope: Exercise has allowed many to lower it.

Men and women deposit fat differently

While men tend to deposit fat on the surface of the skin, women (particularly in their 20's and 30's) fill up internal storage areas first. Young women use the "pinch test" to check fat levels and aren't concerned until the hidden fat areas are somewhat full and the fat spills on to the surface of the body.

A common woman's complaint in the 30's or early 40's is the following: "My body has betrayed me—just during the past year I've been adding fat." In fact, fat has been deposited at a fairly consistent rate but hidden from view for many years. With many women, it is only when the internal fat storage areas are filled that they notice surface fat buildup.

Men find it easier to burn fat than women

When men start exercising regularly, many lose fat and weight for several months. Probably related to biological issues, and primitive protections for mothers, women have a harder time burning it off. The reality is that you are ahead of the others in our society....even if you are maintaining the same weight. Set point increase for an average 45 year old woman in the US would indicate a gain of 3-4 pounds a year. Regular exercise (including taking more walking steps throughout the day) commonly allows women to hold the set point steady for years, and this is a victory. In other words, the set point may be controlled even if you are holding at the same weight, year to year.

Restrictive diets don't work because of the "starvation reflex"

We are certainly capable of lowering food intake for days, weeks and months to lower fat levels and weight. This is a form of starvation and the set point has a long-term memory. Let's say that we lose those 10 pounds during the 2 months before the class reunion. Then, when the diet ends, you'll experience a starvation reflex: a slight increase in appetite and hunger, over weeks and months until the fat accumulated on your body is higher that it was before the diet. It's a fact that almost all of those who lose fat on a diet put more pounds back (than they lost) within months of diet termination.

Waiting too long to eat triggers the starvation reflex

When you wait more than 3 hours without eating something, your set point organism senses that you may be going into a period of starvation. The longer you wait to eat, the more you will feel these three effects of the starvation reflex:

1. A reduction in your metabolism rate: drowsy, lazy, no energy. Imagine an internal voice saying something like this "if this person is going to start depriving me of food I had better tune down the metabolism rate to conserve resources". A slower metabolism means that you have no energy to exercise or move around.

2. An increase in the fat-depositing enzymes. The longer you wait to eat something, the more enzymes you will have, and the more fat will be actually deposited from your next meal.

3. Your appetite increases. The longer you wait to eat, the more likely it is that, for the next few meals, you will have an increased appetite: You're still hungry after a normal meal.

True Ice Cream Confessions (from Jeff)

(An example of the starvation reflex)

Barbara and I used to like a particular type of ice cream so much that we ate a quart or more of it, several nights a week. It was the reward we gave ourselves for reaching exercise goals for that day. Then, on a fateful New Year's Day, we decided to eliminate the chocolate chip mint ice cream from our diet—after more than 10 years of enjoyment. We were successful for 2 years. A leftover box after a birthday party got us restarted on the habit, and we even increased our intake over what it had been before—due to having deprived ourselves.

You can "starve" yourself of a food that you dearly love for an extended period of time. But at some time in the future, when the food is around and no one else is…..you will tend to over-consume that food. Jeff's correction for this problem was the following:

1. I made a contract with myself: I could have a little of it whenever I wanted—while promising to be "reasonable".

2. Setting a goal of enjoying one bowl a week, 5 years from now

3. Four years from now, enjoying a bowl every 5 days

4. Three years from now, a bowl every 4 days

5. Learning to enjoy healthy sweet things, like fruit salads, energy bars, etc., as replacements.

It worked! I hardly ever eat any ice cream…but sometimes enjoy a bowl if I want. This is purely for medicinal reasons, you understand.

Low-carb diets can be a scam

Low-carb diets produce, primarily, a water weight loss—not a fat loss. The lack of sufficient carbohydrate causes a relatively quick loss of 10-25 pounds due to not restocking the glycogen (fuel stored in the muscle that is needed for exercise) and water to service the glycogen. The fat and extra protein in low-carb diets usually adds fat to the body during the low-carb diet, while the water weight loss is registered by the scales. When the dieter goes back to eating carbohydrate again, the water and glycogen weight returns and the added fat is then noticed with a weight gain.

This is a type of starvation diet. I've heard from countless low-carb victims who admit that while they were on the diet, their psychological deprivation of carbs produced a significant rebound effect when they began eating them again. The cravings for bread, pastries, french fries, soft drinks, and other pound-adding foods increased for months after they went off the diet. The weight goes back on, and on, and on.

- Dieting usually triggers the starvation reflex—eating small meals frequently burns more calories

- Caffeine helps in fat burning—but don't take it if you have problems with caffeine

- Find foods that make you feel satisfied, with moderate or lower calorie content

Your Fat Burning Tool Kit

THESE SIMPLE TOOLS WILL GIVE YOU CONTROL OVER THE FAT BURNING PROCESS.

BMI This is a calculation that allows you to monitor your fat increase or reduction, telling you whether you are gaining fat or losing it, whether you are "normal", overweight or obese

Websites or nutritional analysis. Programs, such as Weight Watchers, and websites/software such as www.fitday.com, www.ediet.com, provide guidance in monitoring the income side of the calorie equation, with nutritional "reality checks". These tools help you budget your calories each day to feel satisfied, have more energy and avoid extra intake. They also tell you whether you are getting the quantities of vitamins, minerals, etc. that you need each day.

Step Counters More steps mean more calories burned. The greatest opportunity for fat burning is in adding steps to your day—walking instead of sitting. Checking your count, several times a day can motivate you to add a few more here, and there. It adds up quickly. Go to a technical running store and pick a quality product (usually less than $38).

Bathroom Scale Weigh in immediately after getting out of bed.

Shoes: Pick one that is comfortable and supportive for the type of foot that you have. See the "Running Store Visit" chapter in this book.

A Journal: Small enough to take with you, while having space to jot down food, steps and other exercise

A Piece of Ribbon: To track the reduction of your waist.

BMI Can Monitor Fat Level

The best way to see how you compare to "normal" levels is by computing your BMI. This is somewhat frustrating because even the best scales will show ups and downs for seemingly no reason. You should look at the trends. Don't get discouraged if the scales don't seem to be cooperating. There will be some days when the scales are up, even when you've increased exercise and reduced calorie intake. If you stay focused on your plan of managing the income and increasing or maintaining exercise level, you will be rewarded. When you increase exercise, you may experience an initial weight gain that is healthy and will help you exercise easier and better (more blood volume, more glycogen for fuel, etc.).

What is the BMI? It is a simple computation of your "body mass index" using current weight and height. This evaluation tool has become an international standard telling most individuals whether they fall within the "normal" range, are overweight, or are obese. A few very lean but muscular individuals may register a BMI that is higher than the "normal" range. If you suspect that you fall in this category, talk to your doctor.

Standardize your weight measurement each day. Use the same scale and weigh yourself right after you awaken, before eating or drinking anything. Keep a chart and write down the weight immediately.

The BMI is the best evaluation tool I've seen for evaluating your fat burning progress. At the end of every month or two, it's good to get a "reality check" by computing your BMI. First, average your weight for the month. Then use one of the computation formulas below.

Adult BMI formula:
Inches/pounds: (weight in pounds) divided by (height in inches, squared) times 703

Example: 100 pound person that is 5 feet tall—100 ÷ 3600 x 703 = 19.52 BMI

Example: 200 pound person that is 5 feet tall—200 ÷ 3600 x 703 = 39.05 BMI

Meters/kilograms: (weight in kilograms) divided by (height in meters, squared)

Example: 100 kilogram person that is 2 meters tall—100 ÷ 4 = 25 BMI

Example: 160 kilogram person that is 2 meters tall—160 ÷ 4 = 40 BMI

- Below 25 BMI is considered "Normal"
- Adults with a BMI of 25 to 29.9 are considered "overweight".
- When the BMI exceeds 30, the classification changes to obese. (Parents should consult with the child's pediatrician before computing BMI.)

*A kilogram is 2.2 pounds
*3.27 feet equal one meter

Websites and Nutritional Analysis programs

Successful fat-burners need to monitor calorie and nutritional intake, in order to maintain control, monitor progress and make adjustments. You can choose from a variety of websites or "hands on" programs (such as Weight Watchers) that offer more support. In either case, one must keep a journal of the food eaten each day: food type or brand and quantity. This report is either logged into a website or reported at the weekly meeting of the program. We have used *www.fitday.com* programs, both online and the software. Other sites are *www.ediet.com*, *www.sparkpeople.com*, *www.calorieking.com*. These services not only give you a running tally of calories in/out, but also note deficiencies of calcium, iron, B vitamins, protein, etc.

Step Counter

Not all step counters are created equal. Many are so inconsistent that you could have 4 of the same brand on your belt, and have a difference at day's end of thousands of steps. It helps to get guidance from a technical running store before buying. Price range for a reliable unit is usually $25-$35. Clip it on your belt and write down the total at the end of the day. Your goal is to register more than 10,000 a day. Every time you take a step, you're burning fat. This instrument tells you how much you're burning.

Bathroom Scale
Most scales tend to be reliable. We suggest doing an internet search to see which scales may be more reliable than others. For our purposes, you only need to record the weight. Immediately after rising in the morning, weigh yourself and write down the result.

Shoes
Shoes are designed to support the way your foot walks or runs. The trained staff at a really good running store in your area can advise you. But first, read the shoe selection chapter in the back of this book.

Journal
This does not have to be a technical product. It should be small enough to carry in a purse or pocket. Studies show that those who write down what they eat tend to reduce the number of calories consumed. When you eat anything, write down the food, quantity or weight, and composition if available or needed. You can also record the number of steps taken each day, the type and duration of other exercise, and any other facts that can help you account for the income/expenditure of calories.

A Piece of Ribbon
Use a piece of light colored ribbon. When you start your fat burning program, Put the ribbon around the smallest section of your waist, usually slightly above your belly button or navel. Mark it, and note the date. Once a month, take out the ribbon, measure and mark with the date.

QUICK CHECK BY THE NUMBERS
(make a chart on your wall and track the data, every 6 months
Weight
BMI
Resting heart rate
Cholesterol
HDL
LDL
Blood sugar—diabetes
Waist measurement

Managing the Calorie Budget

"Those who write down everything eaten tend to reduce the quantity of the bad foods."

In this chapter you'll learn the simple steps of tracking the calories eaten each day. If you will stay with the program for a week or two, you'll get more and more efficient in processing the information, and monitoring the data. You will understand where the calories are coming from, which foods are your "prime offenders" and which nutrients you neglect—so that you can supplement as needed.

True confessions: it is initially frustrating to write everything down and then to enter it into the website or notebook at the end of the day. You will get used to this. Within two weeks, most women realize that this is the most important part of calorie management. Knowledge can give you power over food intake— and journaling is a great tool to gain control.

Most women we've known who cannot control their weight don't use a journal. Once you go through the analysis for a few weeks you can look at a food on a shelf or in a menu and guess very accurately the calorie content and the breakdown of many nutrients. You may still eat some or all of the food—but you'll know what you're doing.

1. Buy a Journal: Carry it everywhere...write down everything you eat! Go to an office supply store or a book store and find a journal format that you like, that fits into your purse, etc.

2. When you eat or drink anything (including water) quickly write down the food eaten before or immediately after consuming it.

3. At first you may need to measure items with a food scale, measuring spoons and cups. Learn portion sizes of your favorite foods. Hint, a "portion" is about the size of your fist, or a deck of playing cards.

WHEN EATING IN RESTAURANTS:
- Go to restaurants where there is a chart or brochure on the nutritional breakdown of the food served.
- In a restaurant, ask if they have a recipe notebook, or nutritional breakdown on their website or in the restaurant.
- When buying ready-to-eat foods in a food store, look at the label.
- Some recipe books will give you an analysis of calorie breakdown and nutrients.
- Many websites have standard items (even fast food) broken down in their software. So you can just enter "1 Taco Bell bean burrito, fresco style" and it will do the accounting for you.

Hint: When you suspect (or realize) that a menu item will put you over the limit, get a "to go" container. When your meal is delivered, put half in the container, immediately.

Set an appointment with yourself, at the end of the day, to spend the time necessary to enter items consumed into your website or food log. If you wait two or three days to enter the items, you'll often forget correct quantities or inadvertently leave out items.

Simple is better. Jot down the food so that you can quickly enter the data in your computer program or food log in the evening. It helps to keep a running estimate of total calories consumed to that point in the day. Just estimate. By going through the data entry and analysis each day you will get better and better at estimating.

10 calories per pound need for basal metabolism

Each day, you will be burning about 10 calories per pound of body weight to carry on the beating of the heart, breathing, brain function, etc. The calories burned during exercise will further increase your calorie burning.—but limit the budget number to the figures in the next section. If you limit your intake to the 10 cal/pound amount, you will not have any extra energy for exercise and will feel hungry all day. Don't try this.

Calorie budget should be increased: choose A or B

The type of exercise
12 calories per pound per day for active women: who walk 2-4 miles everyday
15 calories per pound per day for very active women: who run 6 miles daily

Or ...

Tabulate by the duration and type of exercise each day. This will be done automatically if you use a website such as www.fitday.com. You can also do this manually by using the table below:

Calorie burning for one hour of exercise	
Weight Lifting	130 calories
Walking (3 mph)	180 calories
Road Cycling (10 mph)	250calories
Stationary Cycling	250 calories
Average Aerobics	280 calories
Advanced Aerobics	400 calories
Rope jumping	450 calories

Rowing machine	400 to 500 calories
Running with walk breaks at 12 min/mi	500 calories
Running with walk breaks at 9 min/mi	700 calories

Daily calorie deficit: no more than 500 calories per day

In general, we recommend that a daily calorie deficit not exceed 500. By eating 6-9 times a day, and increasing the step count, it is possible to sustain this deficit for several weeks.

Example: A woman who weights 140 pounds has a budget of 1400 calories, when sedentary, 1680 when active and 2100 if very active.

If she eats this allotment every day, and walks for 5000 steps a day separate from workouts, she will burn off about 2.5 pounds a month. Those who eat 6-8 times a day don't tend to run out of energy, feel tired, or feel like they are depriving themselves of food.

Daily Eating Sessions:

In the next chapter we will get into specific food choices at various times of the day. Below are the time periods when it is productive for most people to eat small meals: about 2-3 hours apart. To determine the amount of calories in each meal, take your daily budget and divide by 8. Feel free to add a few calories to some meals, such as breakfast or dinner, and subtract the same amount from the other meals.

Breakfast
Mid Morning
Lunch
Mid Afternoon
Pre workout—100 calories
Post workout—100-150 calories
Dinner
Post Dinner

During each of your eating sessions, write down the food, amount and brand name, if appropriate. Later, you can log these items into your software. We use www.fitday.com software. Whether you use this or another accounting program, or crunch the numbers yourself, try to log it at the end of each day. Waiting longer than this often results in an inaccurate total. Accurate data can give you the power to make changes and manage your eating.

The Eating Plan: Meal by Meal
By Barbara Galloway

Jeff and I are your food coaches. We are not certified dieticians. We will offer proven strategies for getting control over eating, consuming energizing meals all day long and expending energy all day long. Nancy Clark, who is a certified dietitian, has information in her section, in this book and in her book *Sports Nutrition Handbook.* For research-oriented information we highly recommend her books and articles.

Eating with a Purpose
1. Know the calorie content and nutrient breakdown of what you're eating (read the label or use a website like *www.fitday.com*).
2. Concentrate on the positive: "I can eat more of (good tasting fruit and crunchy vegetables") rather than "I have to eat less of _____".
3. Visualize the food on your plate as being in your stomach. Ask yourself, "Do I want to stretch my stomach to cram in more food?" and "Do I need that much right now?"
4. Don't have more than 3 items or "dishes" at one meal.
5. Use spices to improve the taste of food. Food that is "spicy" tends to leave you feeling more satisfied.
6. Drink a glass of water (6-8 oz) before eating, and drink 4-6 oz during the meal.
7. Hot fluids (tea, coffee, broth) leave you feeling fuller than cold fluids.

8. Never eat fatty appetizers if you are very hungry before a meal. Instead, choose soup, salad, hot tea or warm skim milk.

9. Take vitamins with a meal and avoid caffeine for half an hour.

10. Don't even think about going to a buffet.

11. Visit the grocery store with a mission. Have a list of exactly what you will buy and only buy what is on the list.

12. Veggies: steam, toast, or stir-fry—or eat them raw or in salads.

13. Use non-fat dressings or spray-on dressings for salads.

14. Eat slowly! Increase the number of chews for each bite—this triggers more satisfaction in the stomach.

15. Count every calorie eaten—it only hurts you to "forget" the amount or certain foods in your totals.

16. Fluid calories add up quickly. Budget your alcohol, fruit juice, etc.

17. Buy the highest quality foods: lean meats, fruits, veggies and whole grain products. These may cost a little more but you'll appreciate the quality, especially when the taste is better. You will feel better about the quality of your nutrition.

18. Herbs and spices can enhance the savory flavor of foods, leaving you satisfied with fewer calories consumed.

19. Try to accumulate your daily quota of vitamins and minerals from food. If your daily analysis of nutrients shows regular deficiencies (based upon the recommended daily allowance, RDA) then find a really good vitamin. Jeff travels a lot and takes Cooper Complete vitamins, designed by Dr. Kenneth Cooper.

20. In choosing a restaurant, check out the websites to find one that breaks down the nutritional composition of the menu items. By planning ahead, you can avoid impulse eating.

21. Another option is to get a nutritional guide when you arrive at the restaurant and analyze it before the waiter takes your order.

22. Try to avoid or severely limit trans fat and saturated fat.

Choices

The following chart has only some of the many options available. Most folks like to choose 1 item during each time period. As you log in the food consumed, you will learn how much you can eat of each food to stay within budget and/or adjust other items. The website of your choice will also tell you whether you are getting the daily amount of protein, dairy/calcium, fruits, vegetables, grains, fiber—that you need. Look at the labels on each product and put one portion in your bowl or on your plate. Remember to drink about 12 oz of water during/after each meal or snack to feel more satisfied. Increased fiber content may also provide a longer feeling of satisfaction.

Note: When eating 6-9 times a day, you will need to cut the portion size of some featured items. Put the extra amount into a container in the refrigerator for use as another snack later so that you don't have to prepare it.

Early Morning (about 300-400 calories)

- Whole grain bread made into French toast with fruit yogurt, juice, or frozen juice concentrate as syrup
- Whole grain pancake with fruit and yogurt
- A portion of Grape Nuts cereal, skim milk, non-fat yogurt and fruit
- A portion of "Barbara's Special Oatmeal" with a 4 oz glass of orange juice
  1/2 cup oatmeal cooked (rolled or steel cut)
  1/4 cup skim milk
  1/2 oz walnuts
  1 tbs dried fruit
  2 tsp brown sugar or 1 tsp of molasses

Calorie Count:
Total Calories: 419
Fat Calories: 103—12 grams
Carbohydrate: 266—67 grams
Protein: 42—11 grams
Fiber: 6 grams

- Eggs & toast with fruit
    2 eggs—(egg beaters or eggland's best)
    2 slices of whole grain bread
    4 oz orange juice
    1 banana, medium apple or a medium orange
Calorie Count:
Total 454
Fat: 94—11 grams
Carb: 264—66 grams
Protein: 73—19 grams
Fiber: 5 grams

- Mavis Lindgren's 8 Grain Power Breakfast
    Mavis was a sickly child and adult who started to exercise in her late 50's and did not have even a cold for decades. She was a wonderful person, ran marathons into her late 80's and gave us this recipe.

1 cup wheat berries—cook 2-3 minutes in boiling water, store in bowl with enough cool water to cover
In a separate cooking pot:
5 1/2 cups of boiling water with 1 tsp of salt in water
1/2 cup rolled oats
1/4 cup each: millet, rolled rye, whole grain brown rice, rolled soy, 1 tsp flax seed
Bring to a boil and simmer for 10 minutes (in double boiler if possible). Let stand overnight.
Next morning, fold in wheat berries and serve with milk, topped with sunflower seeds, banana, dates, peanuts, granola or whatever you want.

- Cereal with milk and fruit
1 serving of Kellogg's Smart Start Healthy Heart cereal
1/2 cup skim milk
1 banana
1/2 cup skim milk
1 teaspoon Hershey's Chocolate Syrup (optional, 50 calories)

Calorie Count
Total: 404
Fat: 10—1 gram
Carb: 333—84 grams
Protein: 48—12 grams
Fiber: 6 grams

Mid Morning (about150-200 calories)

- Non-fat cottage cheese with fruit
- Whole grain bread, bagel, etc.
- Fat-free yogurt with nuts and fruit
- A small bowl of whole grain cereal with fruit
- An energy bar

Noon (about 400 calories)

- Tuna fish sandwich, whole grain bread, fat-free mayo, coleslaw (with fat-free dressing)
- Turkey breast sandwich with salad, mustard or ketchup or fat-free mayo, celery & carrots
- Veggie burger on whole grain bread, fat-free mayo, salad of choice
- Spinach salad with peanuts, sunflower seeds, almonds, low-fat cheese, non-fat dressing, whole grain rolls or croutons

- Soup & Salad
  1 cup soup, example: Veggie Black Bean
  1 cup tortilla chips—low-fat
  Salad: 2 cups mixed salad greens
             4 cherry tomatoes
             4 cucumber slices
             2 rings bell pepper
             3 baby carrots
             2 tsp low-fat salad dressing
             12 oz non-sweetened tea or a diet drink
Calorie Count
Total: 340

Fat: 106—12 grams
Carb: 198—50 grams
Protein: 36—9 grams
Fiber—10 grams

- Baked Potato with Veggie Chile
  1 medium baked potato about 3 inches in diameter
  1 lemon (vitamin C) to flavor the potato
  1 cup veggie chili with beans (Hormel)
Total: 415
Calorie Count:
Fat: 9—1gram
Carb: 331—83 grams
Protein: 60—15 grams
Fiber: 15 grams

Mid Afternoon (about 150-200 calories)

- microwave cup of soup
- 1/2 peanut butter sandwich—one slice of whole grain bread with peanut butter
- energy bar
- small salad and one cup of fat-free cottage cheese

- Turkey Sandwich (recommend cutting in half, and refrigerating the other half for the next day)
  3 oz of turkey breast slices
  2 slices of whole wheat bread
  2tsp of low-fat mayo
  1 oz Swiss cheese (1 slice)
  4 spinach leaves
  1 tomato slice
Calorie Count (based upon a whole sandwich)
Total: 483
Fat: 200—25 grams
Carb: 118—30 grams
Protein: 163—41
Fiber: 4 grams

- Peanut Butter sandwich with apple and milk (if you will miss lunch)
  1 slice of whole grain bread
  1 tbs peanut butter
  1/2 medium size apple, sliced
  1/2 cup skim milk
Calorie Count:
Total: 286
Fat: 81—9 grams
Carb: 143—36 grams
Protein: 50—13 grams
Fiber: 6 grams

Pre-Workout Snack (about 150 calories)

- Energy Bar
- Toast with honey or jam (no butter or margarine)
- Cup of coffee
- ...or, if you did not eat the pre-workout snack and are a bit hungry, drink about 100-150 calories of Accelerade.

Post-Workout Snack (within 30 minutes of finishing) about 100-200 calories

- 200 calories of Endurox R4 drink (from powder)
- or 200 calories of Accelerade Sports Drink
- or an energy bar that has less than 15% of the calories in fat

Dinner (about 400-500 calories)

There are lots of great recipes in publications such as COOKING LIGHT, and websites such as *www.ediet.com www.epicurous.com*, *www.allrecipes.com*. The basics are listed below. What make the meals come alive are the seasonings which are listed in the recipes. You can use a variety of fat substitutes.

- Fish or lean chicken breast or tofu (or other protein source) with whole wheat pasta, and steamed vegetables

- Rice with vegetables, and a protein source

- Dinner salad with lots of different vegetables, nuts, lean cheese or turkey, fish, chicken or tofu

- Chicken or tofu kabob with brown rice and cooked spinach
  4 oz chicken breast or tofu
  1 cup cooked brown rice
  1 cup cooked spinach
  Pam or similar cooking spray

Calorie Count:
Total: 493
Fat: 110—13 grams
Carb: 209—29 grams
Protein: 174—44 grams
Fiber—8

- Gazpacho

Our friend Linda Kappel gave us this recipe which can be a meal in itself with some whole grain bread.

  1 clove garlic
  1/2 small onion
  1 stalk celery
  1/2 small green pepper
  3 large tomatoes, peeled
  1 medium cucumber, peeled
  1-1 1/2 cups tomato or vegetable juice
  3 tsp wine vinegar
  2 tsp olive oil
  1 1/2 tsp salt
  1/2 tsp dried basil
  1/4 tsp pepper
  dash tabasco

Place all ingredients (in order listed) into food processor. Process on high speed until desired consistency is reached. Chill.

- popcorn
- a piece of chocolate
- a glass of wine
- a glass of water

Practical Eating Issues

Eating every 2-3 hours may burn off 8-10 pounds a year

If you have not eaten for about 3 hours, your body senses that it is going into a starvation mode, and slows down the metabolism rate, while increasing the production of fat-depositing enzymes. This means that you will not be burning as many calories as is normal, that more of your next meal will be stored as fat, and you probably won't be as mentally and physically alert as you could be.

Burn more fat by eating more often—what a deal! If the starvation reflex starts working after 3 hours, then think about eating every 2 hours. A person who now eats 2-3 times a day, can burn 8-10 extra pounds a year when she shifts to eating 6-9 times a day. This assumes equal calories are eaten under each meal frequency pattern.

Big meals slow you down

Big meals are a big production for the digestive system. Blood is diverted to the long and winding intestine and the stomach. Because of the workload, the body tends to reduce blood flow to other areas, leaving you feeling more lethargic.

Small meals speed you up

Smaller amounts of food can usually be processed quickly without putting a burden on the digestive system. Each time you eat a small meal or snack, your metabolism revs up. A metabolism increase, several times a day means more calories burned. At the same time, you'll experience more sustained energy for the next hour or two.

Eating frequently helps you manage the set point
When you wait more than three hours between meals, the set point engages the starvation reflex. But if you eat every 2-3 hours, the starvation reflex is often not engaged—due to the regular supply of food.

Motivation increases when you eat more often
Low motivation in the afternoon is often due to not eating regularly enough during the day: not eating breakfast, not eating enough total calories, and eating very little from lunch until afternoon workout time. If you have not eaten for 4 hours or more, and you're scheduled for a workout that afternoon, you will often not feel very motivated—because of low blood sugar and low metabolism. You can turn this around, even when you've had a bad eating day, by having a snack 30-60 minutes before exercise. A fibrous energy bar with a cup of coffee (tea, diet drink) can reverse the negative mindset and energy deficit. Eating breakfast and then eating every 2-3 hours can keep your energy flowing.

Satisfaction from a small meal—to avoid overeating
The number of calories you eat per day can be reduced by choosing foods and combinations of foods that leave you satisfied longer. Sugar is the worst problem food in calorie control and satisfaction. When you drink a beverage with sugar in it, the sugar will be processed very quickly, and you will often be hungry within 30 minutes—even after consuming a high quantity of calories. This will usually lead to three undesirable outcomes:

1. Eating more food to satisfy hunger.
2. Staying hungry and triggering the starvation reflex.
3. The extra calories are processed into fat.

Your mission is to find the right combination of foods in your small meals that will leave you satisfied for 2-3 hours. Then, eat another snack that will do the same. You will find a growing number of food combinations that probably have fewer calories, but keep you from getting hungry until your next snack.

Nutrients that leave you satisfied longer:

Fat

Fat is automatically deposited on your body. None of the dietary fat is used for energy. When you eat a fatty meal, you might as well inject the fat grams onto your hips or stomach. The fat you burn as fuel must be broken down from the stored fat on your body. So it helps to eat a little fat in a snack (for satisfaction) but too much of it will mean more fat on your body.

A certain amount of fat in a snack or meal will leave you satisfied longer because it slows down digestion, but a little goes a long way. Each gram of fat eaten is deposited on your body—so you want to budget your fat calories. When the fat percentage of a meal (fat calories compared with total calories in the meal) goes beyond 30%, you start to feel more lethargic because fat is harder to digest. Generally it's best to shoot for 15-20% of the calories in a snack to come from fat.

Bad Fat: There are two kinds of fat that have been found to cause narrowing of the arteries around the heart and leading to your brain: saturated fat and trans fat. Mono and unsaturated fats, from vegetable sources, are often healthy—olive oil, nuts, avocado, and safflower oil. Some fish oils have Omega 3 fatty acids which have been shown to have a protective effect on the heart. Many fish have oil that is not protective—so check this out. Most of the fat in animal products is saturated fat.

Look carefully at the labels because a lot of prepared foods have vegetable oils that have been processed into trans fat. A wide range of baked goods and other foods have trans fat. It helps to check the labels, and call the 800 number to ask about foods that don't break down the fat composition. Another simple solution is to simply avoid the foods that aren't well-labeled—especially baked goods.

Protein—go for lean!

You need protein every day, for rebuilding the muscle that is broken down during exercise, as well as normal wear and tear. But endurance exercisers (even runners who log high mileage) don't need to eat significantly more protein than sedentary people. But if endurance exercisers don't get their usual amount of protein, they'll feel more aches and pains (and general weakness) sooner than average people.

Having protein with each meal will leave you feeling satisfied for a longer period of time. But eating more protein calories than you need will produce a conversion of the excess into fat. A general guideline for daily intake of protein is one half a gram for every pound of body weight (or 0.9 grams of protein for each kilogram of body weight).

Recently, protein has been added to sports drinks with great success. When a drink with 80% carbohydrate and 20% protein (such as Accelerade) is consumed within 30 minutes prior to exercise, glycogen is better activated, and energy is supplied sooner. By consuming a drink that has the same ratio (like Endurox R4) within 30 minutes of finishing a workout, the reloading of the muscles has been shown to be more effective.

Complex carbohydrates give you a "discount" and a "grace period"

Foods such as celery, beans, cabbage, spinach, turnip greens, grape nuts, whole grain cereal, etc., can burn up to 25 % of the calories in digestion. As opposed to fat (which is directly deposited on your body after eating it) only the excess carbs are processed into fat. After dinner, for example, you have the opportunity to burn off any excess that you acquired during the day with by walking around the neighborhood. The extra fiber in these foods leaves you satisfied longer.

Fat + Protein + Complex Carbs = SATISFACTION

Eating a snack that has a variety of the three satisfaction ingredients above, will lengthen the time that you'll feel satisfied—even after small meals. These three items take longer to digest, and therefore keep the metabolism rate revved up.

Other important nutrients...

Fiber

When fiber is put into foods, it slows down digestion and maintains the feeling of satisfaction longer. Soluble fiber, such as oat bran, seems to bestow a longer feeling of satisfaction than insoluble fiber such as wheat bran. But any type of fiber will help in this regard.

Recommended percentages of the three nutrients:

There are differing opinions on this issue. Here are the ranges given by a number of top nutritionists that I have read and interviewed. These are listed in terms of the percentage of the daily total of calories in each nutrient.

Protein: between 15% and 25%
Fat: between 15% and 25%
Carbohydrate: whatever is left—hopefully in complex carbohydrates.

Simple Carbohydrates help us add fat

These are the "feel good" foods: candy, baked sweets, starches like mashed potatoes and rice, sugar drinks (including fruit juice and sports drinks) and most desserts. Some simple carbs are good when consumed within 30 minutes of finishing a strenuous workout. But when you're on a fat burning mission you need to minimize the amount of these foods. Again, this is simply a matter of budgeting.

The sugar in these products is digested so quickly that you get little or no lasting satisfaction from them. They often leave you with a craving for more of them, which, if denied, will activate a starvation reflex. Because they are processed quickly, you become hungry relatively quickly and will eat, accumulating extra calories that usually end up as fat at the end of the day.

As mentioned in the last chapter, it is never a good idea to eliminate all of the simple carb foods that you like. The worst situation is to say "I'll never eat another..." This starts the ticking of a starvation-reflex time bomb: at some point in the future, when the food is around and no one else is, you will eat and eat. Keep taking a bite or two of the foods you dearly love when you have cravings—but only a bite or two. At the same time, cultivate an appreciation for the taste of foods with more fiber and little or no refined sugar (and a reduced amount of fat).

Good Blood Sugar = Motivation

Your blood sugar level (BSL) determines how good you feel. When it is at an adequate, moderate level you feel stable, energized, and motivated. If you eat too much sugar, starch or other simple carbohydrate your BSL can rise too high. You'll feel

really good for a while. But the excess sugar triggers a release of insulin that usually pushes BSL too low. In this state, your energy level drops, mental focus is hazy, and motivation can be a problem.

When BSL is maintained at a stable level throughout the day, you will be more motivated to exercise, and will welcome adding other movement to your life. You'll have a more positive mental attitude, and be more likely to deal with stress, and solve problems. Just as eating throughout the day maintains metabolism, the steady infusion of balanced nutrients all day long will maintain stable blood sugar.

You don't want to get on the "bad side" of your BSL. Low levels are a stress on the system and literally mess with your mind. Your brain is fueled by blood sugar and when the supply goes down, your mental stress goes up. If you have not eaten for several hours before a workout, you'll receive an increase in the number of negative messages saying you don't have the energy to exercise, that it will hurt, etc.

The simple act of eating a snack, 30 minutes or less before your workout (containing simple carbohydrate and about 20% protein) will reduce the negative, improve attitude, and help you to get out the door. Keeping a snack as a BSL booster can often determine whether you work out that day or not.

The BSL Roller Coaster

Eating a snack with too many calories of simple carbohydrate can be counter-productive for BSL maintenance. As mentioned above, when the BSL gets too high, your body produces insulin, resulting in a BSL drop. The tendency is to eat again, which results in excess calories consumed—which are converted into fat. But if you don't eat, you'll stay hungry and pretty miserable—in no mood to exercise or move around.

Eating every 2-3 hours is best

When exercisers experiment with various snacks, most find that an individualized arrangement of small meals produces a more level BSL. As noted in the previous chapter, it's best to combine complex carbs with protein and a small amount of fat to achieve this result.

Do I have to eat before a workout? Only if your blood sugar is low

Most people who exercise in the morning don't need to eat anything before the start. As mentioned above, if your blood sugar level is low in the afternoon, and you have a workout scheduled, a snack can help when it is taken about 30 minutes before. If you feel that a morning snack will help, the only issue is to avoid consuming so much that you get an upset stomach.

For best results in raising blood sugar when it is too low (within 30 minutes before exercise) a snack should have about 80% of the calories in simple carbohydrate and 20% in protein. This promotes the production of insulin which is helpful in getting the glycogen in your muscles ready for use. The product Accelerade has worked best among the thousands of exercisers I hear from every year. It has the 80%/20% ratio of carb to protein. If you eat an energy bar with the 80/20 ratio, be sure to drink 6-8 oz of water at the same time.

Eating during exercise

Most exercisers don't need to worry about eating or drinking during a workout until the length of the session exceeds 60 minutes (for most of my clients, 90 minutes). At this point, there are several options. Most will wait until they have been exercising for about 40 minutes before starting to take the first booster snack—but this time will vary between individuals. Practice various eating strategies on your long workouts, and pick what works best.

Gel products—these come in small packets, and are the consistency of honey or thick syrup. The most successful way to take them is to put 1-2 packets into a small plastic bottle with a pop-top. About every 10-15 minutes, take a squirt or two, with a sip or two of water.

Energy Bars—Cut a bar into 8-10 pieces and take a piece, with a couple of sips of water, every 10-15 minutes.

Candy—particularly gummi bears. The usual consumption is 2-4 small units, about every 10-15 minutes.

Sports Drinks—Since there is a significant percentage of nausea among those who drink these during exercise, this is not my top recommendation. If you have found that a product works for you, use it exactly as you have used it before.

It is important to re-load after exercise—within 30 minutes

Whenever you have finished a hard or long workout (for you), a reloading snack of 100-200 calories will help you recover faster. Again, the 80%/20% ratio of carb to protein has been most successful in reloading the muscles. The product that has worked best among the thousands I work with each year is Endurox R4.

Nutrition Advice from Nancy Clark

One of the foremost experts in nutrition for exercise

Myth: You must exercise in order to lose body fat

To lose body fat, you must create a calorie deficit. You can create that deficit by adding exercise (which improves your overall health and fitness) or by eating fewer calories. Sick people commonly lose body fat but they do not exercise; they create a calorie deficit. Similarly, injured athletes can also lose fat despite lack of exercise. But the more common story is the following. "I gained weight when I was injured because I couldn't exercise," could more correctly be stated, "I gained weight when I was injured because I was bored and depressed. I over ate for comfort and entertainment..."

Myth: The more you exercise, the more fat you lose

Often, the more you exercise, the hungrier you get and

- the more you eat, or
- the more your believe you "deserve" to eat, or
- the more you want to eat as a reward for having both gotten to the gym and survived the exercise session.

But if you spend 60 minutes in a spin class and burn off 600 calories, only to reward yourself with twelve Oreos (600 calories), you quickly wipe out your weight loss efforts in less than 3 minutes...

The effects of exercise on weight loss are complex and unclear. We know among older people (56-78 years) who participated in a vigorous walking program, daily calorie needs remained about the same (2,400 without exercise, 2,480 with exercise). How could that be? Well, the participants napped more and were 62% less active throughout the rest of their day. (1)

Another study with post-menopausal women found the same results from 8 weeks of moderate exercise training. Their 24-hour energy expenditure remained similar from the start to the end of the program. (2) The bottom line: You have to eat according to your whole day's activity level, not according to how hard you trained that day.

Myth: If you train for a marathon, your body fat will melt away

Wishful thinking. I commonly hear marathoners, triathletes and other highly competitive endurance athletes complain "For all the exercise I do, I should be pencil thin..." They fail to lose fat because, like the fitness exercisers described above, they put all of their energy into exercising, but then tend to be quite sedentary the rest of the day as they recover from their tough workouts. A study with male endurance athletes who reported a seemingly low calorie intake found they did less spontaneous activity than their peers in the non-exercise parts of their day. (3) The bottom line: you need to keep taking the stairs instead of the elevators, no matter how much you train!

Alternatively, athletes who complain they eat like a bird but fail to lose body fat may simply be under-reporting their food intake. A survey of female marathoners indicated the fatter runners under-report their food intake more so than their leaner peers. (4) Remember: calories mindlessly eaten standing up or on-the-run count just as much as calories from meals.

Myth: Couples who exercise together lose fat together

In a 16-month study looking at exercise for weight loss, men and women completed an identical amount of exercise. The men lost 11.5 pounds; the women maintained weight! (5) In another study with previously sedentary, normal weight men and women who participated in an 18 month marathon training program, the men increased their calorie intake by about 500 per day; the women increased by only 60 calories—despite having added on 50 miles per week of running. The men lost about five pounds of fat; the women two pounds. (6)

What's going on here??? Well, a husband who adds on exercise is likely to lose more weight than his wife because he's likely heftier and thereby burns more calories during the same workout. But, speaking in terms of evolution, Nature seems protective of women's role as child bearer, and wants women to maintain adequate body fat for nourishing healthy babies. Hence, women are more energy efficient. Obesity researchers at NY's Columbia University suggest a pound of weight loss in men equates to a deficit of about 2,500 calories, while women need a 3,500 calorie deficit!!! (7) No wonder women have a tougher time losing weight then do men....

The bottom line

If you are exercising to lose weight, I encourage you to separate exercise and weight. Yes, you should exercise for health, fitness, stress relief and, most importantly, for enjoyment. (After all, the E in exercise stands for enjoyment!) I discourage you from exercising to burn off calories; that makes exercise feels like punishment for having excess body fat. When exercise is something you do to your body, rather than do for your body, you'll eventually quit exercising. Bad idea. Pay attention to your calorie intake. Knocking off just 100 calories a day from your evening snacks can theoretically result in 10 pounds a year of fat loss. Seems simpler than hours of sweating...?

References:
1. Goran, *Am J Physiol* 263:E950, 1992
2. Keytel, *Int J Sport Nutr* 11:226, 2001
3. Thompson, *Med Sci Sports Exerc* 27:347, 1995
4. Edwards, *Med Sci Sports Exer* 25:1398, 1993
5. Donnelly, *Arch Intern Med* 163:1343, 2003
6. Janssen, *Int J Sports Med*, 10:S1,1989
7. Pietrobelli *Int J Obes Relat Metab Disord* 26:1339, 2002

Taming the Cookie Monster

By Nancy Clark

"I know I shouldn't eat cookies–but I just can't help myself. I'm a cookie monster!"
Sound familiar? Everyone knows that cookies (and candy, cakes, pies, ice cream, other sweets) offer suboptimal nutrition. But why are cookies so popular? Why do we eat monstrous portions that were not a part of our food intentions?

Why? Because cookies (and other sweets) taste good. Because athletes–or anyone, for that matter–who get too hungry tend to crave sweets. Most athletes believe cookies are the problem. I challenge that belief. I see cookies as being the symptom and getting too hungry as being the problem. That is, when you get too hungry, you experience a very strong drive to eat. Cookies!!!

Hunger, a simple request for fuel

Hunger is a very powerful physiological force that creates a strong desire to eat. When a child complains about being hungry, the parent readily provides food. But when athletes experience hunger, they either have „no time" to eat or, if weight-conscious, they fear food as being fattening; eating equates to getting fat.

Most athletes eat without getting fat. Food, after all, is fuel. But cookie monster problems arise when time-deprived or dieting athletes consume inadequate fuel and hunger becomes the norm. The result is an abnormal physiological state known as starvation –or more commonly, known as being „on a diet". Although starvation is associated with famine in poor countries, starvation is also common among busy and dieting athletes.

In 1950, Ancel Keys and his colleagues at the University of Minnesota studied the physiology of starvation. They carefully monitored 36 young, healthy, psychologically normal men who for 6 months were allowed to eat only half their normal intake

(similar to a very restrictive reducing diet). For 3 months prior to this semi-starvation diet, the researchers carefully studied each man's behaviors, personality, and eating patterns. They also observed the men for three to nine months of refeeding.

As the subjects' body weight fell, the researchers learned that many of the symptoms that might have been thought to be specific to binge eating were actually the result of starvation. The most striking change was a dramatic increase with food preoccupation. The hungry subjects thought about food all the time. They talked about it, read about it, dreamed about it, even collected recipes. They dramatically increased their consumption of coffee and tea, and chewed gum excessively. They became depressed, had severe mood swings, experienced irritability, anger and anxiety. They became withdrawn and lost their sense of humor. They had cold hands and feet, and felt weak and dizzy. During the study, some of the men were unable to maintain control over food; they would binge eat if the opportunity presented itself—similar to "breaking a diet" or bingeing on cookies.

When the study ended and the men could eat freely, many of them ate continuously—big meals followed by snacks. They ate and ate—like a cookie monster. So what can we learn about binge-eating from this study?

1. Preoccupation with cookies (and sweets) indicates your body is too hungry. Hunger creates a strong physiological drive to eat.

2. Cookie binges stem from starvation. If you are unable to stop eating once you start, you have likely gotten monstrously hungry (or are very stressed).

3. Dieters who restrict to the point of semi-starvation are likely to "blow their diets" and consequently acquire some benefits: less hunger, cookies (and other sweets), and more energy.

Living without hunger

In our society, people live in hunger because the prevailing messages are "I don't have time to eat" and "food is fattening." Athletes believe the best way to lose weight is to severely restrict calories. The only opportunity dieters have to eat cookies (and other tasty foods) is when they "blow" their diets and turn into cookie monsters. But there is another way to manage cookies:

1. prevent hunger by eating enough at meals. You can lose weight by eating 10% to 20% fewer calories, not 50% fewer.

2. enjoy a cookie or two as a part of an overall healthful daily food plan.

To know how many calories (and cookies) you are entitled to eat to negate hunger and manage your weight, do this simple math:

- Take your weight (or a good weight for your body) and multiply it by 10. This estimates your resting metabolic rate (RMR, the amount of energy you need to simply exist, pump blood, breathe, etc.). If you weigh 140 pounds, your RMR is about 1,400 calories—the amount you'd burn if you were to run for 14 miles!

- Add to your RMR about half that number for activities of daily living. For example, if you weigh 140 pounds and are moderately active (without your purposeful exercise), you need about 700 calories for daily living. Add fewer calories if you are sedentary.

- Next, add calories for purposeful exercise. For example, a 140 lb person would need about 1,400 calories (RMR) + 700 (daily living) + 300 (for 30 minutes of exercise) = 2,400 calories to maintain weight. To lose weight, deduct 20%, to about 1,900 calories. This translates into 600 calories for breakfast/snack, 700 for lunch/snack, and 600 for dinner/snack (or the equivalent of 11-13 Fig Newtons per section of the day.)

The next time you get into a cookie frenzy, use food labels to calculate your day's intake. You'll likely see a huge discrepancy between what you have eaten and what your body deserves. No wonder you are craving cookies! Once you recognize the power of hunger, you can take steps to prevent it by eating before you get too hungry.

Living with cookies

If you like cookies too much—to the extent you have trouble stopping eating them once you start—the way to take the power away from cookies is to eat them more often (in appropriate portions) and not try to "stay away from them." Apples likely have no "power" over you because you give yourself permission to eat an apple whenever you want. But cookies will have power over you if you routinely restrict them. By enjoying a cookie with every lunch, you'll start to want fewer cookies. They will lose their appeal and the cookie monster will rest in its cage, peacefully.

Nancy Clark, MS, RD counsels sports-active people at Healthworks (617-383-6100) in Chestnut Hill MA. Her Sports Nutrition Guidebook, Third Edition ($19.95) and her Food Guide for Marathoners ($16.95) have more information on weight control. Send a check to Sports Nutrition Services, PO Box 650124, Newton MA 02465 or visit www.nancyclarkrd.com.

Exercise Is Fun!
If You Stay in the Fat-burn Zone

What Do You Need to Get Started?
The Best Fat Burning Exercises
Your First Week: How to Begin and Continue
Training Program: The Next 3 Weeks
The Next 22 Weeks
How to Burn Up to 65 Pounds a Year
Eating for Exercise

Note: Be sure to see the following:

What Do You Need to Get Started?

There are a growing number of "things" that can help make exercise easier: shoes, clothing, a training journal, watches, water belts, sun glasses, etc. The choice of bras is detailed in the woman's exercise issues on page 26. As running store owners, we're very pleased that these items make exercise easier and more fun. But most exercises don't require much equipment to get started. Your top priority should be to enjoy the exercise experience. Focus on finding shoes, clothing and equipment that make you comfortable during your workout.

Medical Check

Check with your doctor's office before you start exercising. Just tell the doctor or head nurse that you plan to start a gentle exercise routine, and have a successful and gentle plan (listed in this book). Almost every person will be given the green light. If your doctor is not in favor of this, ask why. Since there are so few people who have problems related to gentle exercise, I suggest that you get a second opinion if your doctor tells you not to exercise. The best medical advisor is one who wants you to regularly exercise in the mode that is realistic for you, and will advise you about medical issues to make this happen.

Heart Disease and Exercise

Exercise tends to offer some protection from cardiovascular disease. But more women exercisers die of heart disease than any other cause, and are susceptible to the same risk factors as sedentary people. Like most other citizens, exercisers at risk usually don't know that they are. Every year, several exercisers who have suffered heart attacks and strokes could probably have prevented them if they had taken a few simple tests. Some of these are listed below, but check with your doctor if you have any questions or concerns.

***Risk Factors—get checked if you have two of these—or one that
your doctor notes as "significant"***

- Family history
- Poor lifestyle habits earlier in life
- High fat/high cholesterol diet
- Have smoked—or still smoke
- Obese or severely overweight
- High blood pressure (Good to be under 135/85, better if under 125/75)
- High cholesterol (Good to be under 180, better if under 150)
- High blood sugar (Good to be under 100)

Tests can tell you if you are at risk

- Stress Test—heart is monitored during a run that gradually increases in difficulty. This test will screen out some at risk, but many with real problems fall through the cracks.

- Cholesterol Screening—A number that is below 180 is good, and below 150 is excellent. Ask your doctor about your individual situation and the variation between your HDL particles (better to have a higher percentage of these) and your LDL (particles that can cause problems).

- C reactive Protein— has been an indicator of increased risk.

- Heart scan—an electronic scan of the heart which shows calcification, and possible narrowing of arteries. A higher than normal reading does not mean blockage but may indicate the need for more tests.

- Radioactive dye test—very effective in locating specific blockages. Talk to your doctor about this.

- Carotid ultrasound test—helps to tell if you're at risk for stroke.

- Ankle-brachial test—denotes plaque buildup in arteries throughout the body.

None of these are foolproof. But by working with your cardiologist, you can increase your chance of living until the muscles just won't propel you further down the road.

Safety

Take charge by thinking ahead and being aware of your surroundings.

- Bring a shrill whistle with you.
- In uncertain areas, bring pepper spray.
- Bring a cell phone, and call someone if you feel threatened.
- Wear an ID tag on your shoe.
- Tell someone where you will be running/walking/exercising, and when you should be back.
- Use your instincts—turn around if you feel uneasy in a certain area.
- Wear white and reflective clothing at night, and run/walk where the streets are well lit.
- Don't take chances in traffic—wait until the traffic is clear to cross the street—look both ways, twice.
- Run/walk facing traffic—and always have an escape route. Assume all drivers are crazy or drunk.
- When running/walking with others, never assume that someone is looking ahead for your safety.
- Best not to wear any device in your ear, but if you do, keep the sound as low as possible and one ear uncovered.
- If threatened, swing your elbow at the head of the attacker, put fingers in the eyes, and kick at the groin.

Shoes: the primary investment:
usually less than $100 and more than $65

It's a good idea to spend a little time on the choice of a good exercise shoe. After all, shoes are one of two most important pieces of equipment needed (bras are the second item). The correct shoe can make exercise easier, and reduce blisters, foot fatigue and injuries. Get the best advice you can from the staff at the best running store in your area. Be sure to tell the staff person the primary exercises you will be doing. See the section on shoe fitting on page .

Clothing: comfort above all
The "clothing thermometer" at the end of this book will tell you what works for most exercisers, at various temperatures. In the summer, you want to wear light, cool clothing. During cold weather, layering is the best strategy. As you get into longer sessions, you will find various outfits that make you feel better and motivate you to get in your workout even on bad weather days. It is also OK to give yourself a fashionable outfit as a "reward" for exercising regularly for several weeks.

A Training Journal
The journal is an important motivation tool. It will also help you set up your training plan and track your progress.

Where to exercise
The best place to start is in your neighborhood—especially if there are sidewalks, health clubs, or home equipment. First priority is safety. Walkers and runners need to pick a course that has some protection from car traffic, and is in a safe area—where crime is unlikely. Variety can be very motivating.

Surface
With the selection of the right shoes for you, pavement usually does not give extra shock to the legs or body. A smooth surface dirt or gravel path is best for most people, but hard to find. Beware of an uneven surface especially if you have weak ankles or foot problems.

Picking an exercise companion
If you are competitive, don't exercise with someone who is at a higher level of performance than you, unless both of you can exercise at your own paces on a walk, run or in the gym. It is

motivating to exercise with someone nearby so that you can talk. Share stories, jokes, problems if you wish, and you'll bond together in a very positive way. The friendships forged during the long sessions can be the strongest and longest lasting—if you're not huffing and puffing (or puking) from trying to maintain a pace that is too difficult.

Rewards

Rewards are important at all times. But they are crucial for most exercisers in the first 3-6 weeks. Be sensitive and provide rewards that will keep you motivated, and make the workout experience a better one (more comfortable shoes, clothes, etc.)

Positive reinforcement works! Treating yourself to a smoothie after a workout, taking a cool dip in a pool, going out to a special restaurant after a longer one—all of these can reinforce the good habit you are establishing. In fact, you'll speed recovery by having a snack, within 30 minutes of the finish, that has about 100-200 calories, containing 80% carbohydrate and 20% protein. The products Accelerade and Endurox R4 are already formulated with this ratio for your convenience, and make good rewards.

An appointment on the calendar

Write down each of your weekly workouts, 2 weeks in advance, on your calendar. Sure you can change if you have to. But by getting the "appointment" secure, you can plan your day, and make it happen. Pretend that this is an appointment with your favorite relative, your boss, or your most important client, etc. Actually, you are your most important client!

Treadmills are just as good as streets

More and more walkers/runners are using treadmills for at least 50% of their runs/walks—particularly women who have small children. It is a fact that treadmills tend to tell you that you have gone further or faster than you really have (usually by no more than 10%). But if you exercise on a treadmill for the number of minutes assigned, at the effort level you are used to (no huffing and puffing), you will get close enough to the training effect you wish. To ensure that you have covered enough miles, feel free to add 10% to your assigned mileage.

Running Strollers

Strollers can give mothers more freedom to run/walk outside, with child or children. There are a number of quality products that make the ride smooth and reduce the effort of pushing one or two kids around. (Yes there are models designed for two.) Try several out, and ask around for used ones. It helps to have one that will fold up and can be put in your car easily, is easy to steer, is comfortable for your child (children), and has a hand strap. Twenty inch wheels (or larger) are generally recommended. Some running clubs and running stores try to match up used stroller-sellers with buyers.

Usually no need to eat before exercise

Most exercisers don't have to eat before sessions that are less than about an hour and a half. The only exceptions are those with diabetes or severe blood sugar problems. Many exercisers simply feel better during a workout when they have enjoyed a cup of coffee (with an energy bar, etc.) about an hour before the start. Caffeine engages the central nervous system, which gets all of the systems needed for exercise up and running to capacity very quickly. Don't take caffeine if you have heart rhythm problems or negative caffeine sensitivities.

If your blood sugar is low, which often occurs in the afternoon, it helps to have a snack of about 100-200 calories within the 30 minute period before exercise that is composed of 80% carbohydrate and 20% protein. The Accelerade product has been very successful.

The Best Fat Burning Exercises

- The best exercises are those that use a great number of muscle cells and don't exhaust the muscles: walking, running, rowing, nordic track type exercise—all done at a gentle pace
- At first, schedule small segments and mix them during a workout, with rest between segments.
- Have several indoor options: exercise machines, mall walking, treadmills, indoor tracks.
- Have several outdoor options: parks, fitness trails, neighborhood courses, swimming pools, etc.
- When you don't feel like exercising, just do 1-3 minutes. Small segments lead to bigger ones.
- Wonderful things happen as we get "In Shape" feeling better and better.
- Stay aerobic! Gentle exercise keeps you in the fat burning zone.
- When you move gently, you burn fat. (When sedentary, strive to walk for 5 minutes every hour throughout the day).
- Best to set a modest goal for the first month. Then re-evaluate. The most important process is enjoying exercise—then you will have more desire to do it again, and again.
- Even if you don't lose a pound, the exercise habit will give you more vitality and mental focus.
- You need energy to feel good, and to fuel muscles during workouts—so don't starve yourself.
- Losing 1-2 pounds a month is realistic. 1-2 pounds a week is very difficult to sustain.
- Realize that you will experience plateaus even when you seem to be doing everything right.
- Be Honest! Beware of false entries—over reporting of exercise and under reporting of intake is common and results in low motivation.
- Choose exercises that you like to do, and are easy to do.
- DON'T GIVE UP! Sidebar end

You are in charge of your exercise

The program that follows will allow exercisers at any current level of fitness to burn fat and increase over 6 months. The first goal, and sign of success, is being consistent: exercising at least 3 times a week: 1) schedule your workouts on your calendar, and 2) exercise gently enough so you'll experience the many rewards immediately.

- Learn to enjoy several exercises—variety increases motivation.

- The best exercises are those that you enjoy doing—you're more likely to do them.

- Exercise machines, or local parks or health clubs, can make exertion more convenient.

Most beneficial fat burn exercise: WALKING

Get a step counter and shoot for at least 10,000 steps a day. This is a fill-in exercise that burns fat all day while making you feel better. When you look at the count, several times a day, you're more likely to insert more steps with each step-check. Record the total at the end of the day in your journal or calendar. When you insert walking steps into the "dead periods" of your day you prop up your energy level and can burn 20-30 pounds off in a year.

Ease into each mode of exercise

Small segments of exercise should not produce soreness, excess fatigue or injury. If you have not been doing a given exercise, recently, start with segments of 2-3 minutes. Take a break from that exercise for at least 2-3 minutes and do a second segment of 2-3 minutes. An initial fat burning workout could be the accumulation of 8-10 minutes of these segments or slightly more. The secret in avoiding soreness is to quit well before you have done too much for you—each day. If you're doing the same exercise every 2-3 days, a safe increase is 1-2 additional minutes on each segment. It is better to stop before you feel tired.

Calorie burning for one hour of exercise

Weight Lifting	130 calories
Walking (3 mph)	180 calories
Road Cycling (10 mph)	250 calories
Stationary Cycling	250 calories
Average Aerobics	280 calories
Advanced Aerobics	400 calories
Rope jumping	450 calories
Rowing machine	400 to 500 calories
Running 12 min/mi	500 calories
Running 9 min/mi	700 calories

Your First Week—
How to Begin and Continue

Note: Be sure to read the section that follows on "How to get started". There are many important items such as heart health and heat, with practical information on shoes, etc.

Three Exercise Days per Week:
• Two sessions during the week
• One longer one on the weekend
• Follow the training schedule below

Exercise in a series of short segments

You can avoid aches, pains and injuries if you start with a short segment of each exercise which does not push muscles beyond their limits. At first it's best to do just 1-2 minutes of exercises that you have not been doing recently. Some will need to alternate one minute of exercise with one minute of gentle walking (exercise machine, etc.) or rest. During the rest break, you can walk gently, in or around a pool (great for summer) or sit down if you really need to do so. When it doubt, reduce the duration of the exercise segments at first. It's best that you not stand around—keep moving the legs or sit down if you need more rest. A 10 minute workout could be structured as follows:

*"Off The Couch" Workout for those who have been very
sedentary*
Walk for 2 minutes, walk gently (see the walk/shuffle chapter)
for 1 minute, walk for 3 minutes, walk gently for 1 minute, walk
for 3 minutes, walk gently for 3 minutes.

Beginning Runner Workout
Gently walk for 2 minutes, during the next 3 minutes insert 5-10
seconds of very gentle running into each minute while walking
comfortably, then take 3 minutes of rest, come back with 3 more
minutes of 5-10 second insertions, followed by 3 minutes of
gentle walking at the end.

*First Workout for those who have done a little exercise during
the last year*
Gently walk for 2 minutes, rowing machine for 2 minutes, walk
gently for 1-2 minutes, exercise cycle for 2 minutes, walk for 1-2
minutes, rowing or swimming for 2 minutes, walk for 1-3 minutes.

Pool Workout
Swim for 2 minutes, gently walk around the shallow end for a
minute, run in the deep water for 2 minutes, walk in the shallow
end for a minute, swim for 2 minutes, walk in shallow end for a
minute, run in the water for a minute.

Venues: Home, Work, Kid's Activity Area...
The easier it is to get out the door, the more likely you will
exercise. The most common venues are the following:

1. Early morning, on your neighborhood walking or jogging
   course, (or home exercise machines) before the rest of the
   family has awakened.
2. At noon, from your worksite or home.
3. A health club that is near either work or home.
4. From work to let traffic die down, from home before other
   family members have arrived—or with friends or family
   members.

5. After dinner—with other family members (not recommended if you have trouble sleeping).
6. When you are waiting for someone. Soccer moms can walk or run around the practice field, for example.

Your pace

Start every segment of each exercise at a slow and gentle pace so that you do not huff and puff—even at the end of the workout. During the first month it is best to maintain an easy pace on all segments so that you will have no problem increasing the segments. When walking or running, keep your feet low to the ground, lightly touching—as in a "shuffle". Don't lift your knees. In general, make it easy on yourself. You want to get into a groove when moving forward so that you don't feel the muscles, feet, joints. This means that everything is working together within a range of motion for which you are designed. Slow and gentle walking or running in short segments, produces few, if any, aches and pains. Long strides, however, will increase the chance of injury or fatigue.

Your effort level: You cannot exercise too easy during the first few workouts!

After several weeks, you can increase effort a bit. Be very conservative for the first few weeks. You don't want to huff and puff at any time, because this means that you are no longer in the fat burning zone.

A Training Journal

You can record your exercise in the same journal used to record food—or choose a separate journal. Many beginners start with one for both. A reward for being regular with exercise is the purchase of a separate training journal. This offers more space for planning, recording results and adding notes for improvement or positive thoughts.

Thursday

GOAL	35 min easy (SC)
TIME	45 min
DISTANCE	@ 6.5
AM PULSE	49
WEATHER	cloudy
TEMP	40°
TIME	6 AM/**PM**
TERRAIN	rolling
DATE	WALK BREAK —

Jan 4

COMMENTS

Great run with Barb, Wes + Sambo — who took out the pace too fast + died at the end. The rest of us caught up on the gossip. Achilles ached so I iced it for 15 minutes.

1 2 3 4 5 6 7 (8) 9 10

Friday

GOAL	45 min (sp) 5 × 800 meter
TIME	1:15
DISTANCE	7.5 mi
AM PULSE	53
WEATHER	45°
TEMP	sunny
TIME	5 AM/**PM**
TERRAIN	track
DATE	WALK BREAK 400 m

Jan 5

COMMENTS

2:30
2:36
2:33 felt
2:37
2:32 Performance
2:36

My best workout in years!
- walked 400m between each
- struggled on last one

Achilles ached - iced 15 min

12 min warm up and warm down

1 2 3 4 (5) 6 7 (8) 9 10

Saturday

GOAL	Off
TIME	
DISTANCE	
AM PULSE	55
WEATHER	
TEMP	
TIME	AM PM
TERRAIN	
DATE	WALK BREAK

Jan 6

COMMENTS

Kids soccer (Morn)
* Westin scores goal bouncing off his back
    1st goal of season!
  Brennan's cross country (aft)
        Invitational
* Brennan comes from 8th to 3rd in the last half mile. I'm so proud!

1 2 3 4 5 6 7 8 9 10

Sunday

GOAL	18 mi (1) easy!
TIME	2:53
DISTANCE	18 mi
AM PULSE	52
WEATHER	50°
TEMP	dry no wind
TIME	AM/PM
TERRAIN	flat
DATE	WALK BREAK 1 min / mi

Jan 7

COMMENTS

It was great to cover 18 miles —
wish I had a group
longest run in 18 months!
        but...
* went too fast in the first 5 miles
* Achilles hurt afterward - take 3 days off
* Power Bar + water from 10 mi kept spirits up

1 2 3 4 5 (6) 7 8 9 10

Pulse is up — I'm not recovering — need more days off/week

THE FIRST WORKOUT

1. Put on a comfortable pair of shoes.

2. Put on light, comfortable clothes—see "clothing thermometer" in this book.
    Note: Clothes don't have to be designed for exercise—just comfortable.

3. Walk for 5 minutes at a very slow pace to warm the muscles up gently.

4. If the legs are moving comfortably and naturally, move into the next segment (exercise of your choice).

5. During each segment, get into a smooth motion that feels very comfortable to you.

6. Make it easy on yourself! During this first session, do only 6-10 minutes, total. ("Getting started" runners will alternate 5-10 seconds of running with 1-2 minutes of walking.)

7. Walk slowly for 5-10 minutes as a "warm-down" after the workout.

8. During each segment, don't push until you are huffing and puffing or feel muscle soreness or pain. Stop each segment thinking you could have gone further. Move from one segment to another in a smooth transition.

9. "Getting started" runners: Read the Run-Walk-Run™ chapter in this book. There is more information in Jeff's book Getting Started.

10. Keeping track of the segments: There are watches that can be programmed to beep at the beginning and end of an exercise segment. For example, if you are exercising for 2 minutes and rest/walking slowly for 2 minutes you can set some watches to beep every 2 minutes. For more info on watches visit *www.JeffGalloway.com*.

Warm-up

By walking for 5 minutes, very slowly, you will gently move the tendons and ligaments through the necessary range of motion. At the same time, you'll send blood into the muscles, as you get the heart, lungs and circulation system ready for gentle exertion. Your nervous system can get into "sync" when you have at least 5 minutes of easy movement as a warm-up. If you need more minutes of slow walking, continue doing so.

What? No stretching?

That's right. We see no reason to stretch before walking or running, unless you have some unusual problem that has been helped by stretching. The Iliotibial band injury is one of these exceptions. Overall, we see many injuries every year that are caused by stretching. Some individuals find that gentle stretching helps them warm up for other types of exercise. Do what works for you.

Breathing—no huffing and puffing

Don't huff and puff. You want to carry on a conversation as you exercise. This is called the "talk test". If you want to do a rowing segment for 2 minutes, but were huffing and puffing at one and a half minutes, stop the rowing at the first sign of huffing and do a slow walk to recover. If you do another rowing segment, reduce the effort level from the beginning.

Warm down

Just walk easily for 5-10 minutes. It is important that you keep moving the legs slowly after the workout. Don't ever go right into the shower after a vigorous exercise session, and don't stand around immediately after a workout because this can be very stressful on your heart. If you want to walk farther and have been walking regularly, go ahead.

The day after

The day after your first workout, take the day off from exercise, or walk gently for a few minutes. After a few weeks you will be able to walk further and further on this easy day.

The second workout

Two days after your first workout, it's time to exercise again. As long as you have recovered quickly from the first day, repeat the same routine as the first time, but extend the number of segments by 1 or 2. If you haven't fully recovered, keep the same number of segments and go more slowly. Beginning runners, keep your stride very short and gentle.

The third workout—two days later

Continue to add to the number of gentle exercise segments by 1 or 2 more than you did in the second workout.

Alternate

Do your workouts about every other day, with a day off between (or a day of easy walking for 2000-5000 steps). As long as the legs and body are recovering, you could continue increasing as noted on the schedules that follow. The warm up and warm down periods can stay the same—or you can add more walking if you feel like doing so.

Regularity

...is extremely important during the first 8 weeks. On a very busy day, if you feel that you don't have time, just walk for 5 minutes. Even this short exercise period will help to maintain most of the adaptations. Naturally it is better to do more than this, but 5 minutes is better than zero. If you wait 3 days between workouts, you start to lose the adaptations, and your body complains a bit longer into each session. Getting into a habit is the most helpful way to make it past 3 weeks—a major stepping stone to fitness success.

Reward Yourself!

After you have finished your first week of three sessions, congratulate yourself with a special exercise outfit, meal, trip to a scenic walk area, etc. Simple rewards can be very powerful.

Congratulations! You're on your way!

Training Program: The Next 3 Weeks

If you settle into your exercise habit during the next three weeks—only 9 sessions—you have about an 80% chance of continuing for 6 months, according to my experience. The members of the "six month club" tend to continue as lifelong exercisers. Here are some tips for your 21 day mission:

- Find a place in your schedule when you normally have time to exercise. For most people this means getting up 30 minutes early. Go to bed 30 minutes early. But even if you don't, you should be fine with 30 min less sleep. The overwhelming response from exercisers we've worked with, who've initially said they couldn't live without those 30 minutes (but gave it a try), is…..they really had no problem. The vitality you gain from your gentle exercise session will energize the rest of your day.

- Get your spouse, significant other, friends, co-workers, etc., to be your support team. Promise that if you get through the next 3 weeks having done each of the workouts (only 9 of them), that you will have a party for them, picnic, whatever. Pick supportive people who will email you, and will reinforce your exercise during and after the training.

- Have a friend or three who you can call, in case you have a low motivation day. Just the voice on the phone can usually get you out the door, or on the treadmill, etc. Of course it is always better to have a positive and enthusiastic person in this role.

- Talk to your kids about what you are doing for yourself: you feel better, you think better, your heart is healthier, and you can do more because you exercise. This plants the seed that exercise is good, that "our family members exercise".

- Have a back-up time to exercise. The usual times for this are at noon or after work.

- While commuter traffic is high, get in your workout: some get to work very early, and others work out immediately after work.
- If necessary, you can break up your exercise time into several segments: morning, lunch hour, after dinner.

- You can choose one exercise or can use a variety of exercises. A table of the average calorie burning by activity is noted in the previous chapter.

- Feel free to walk gently on the "off" days. Walk with a short stride.

- Suggestions for running and walking are included only for those would like to use my run-walk-run™ method to get into running. Disregard this if you are doing other exercises.

- Based upon genetics and exercise background, some will be able to progress more quickly than others. It is always better to be conservative—and go at your own pace.

Remember, no huffing and puffing!

Summary:
The First 4 Weeks

Time noted is the total # of minutes of exercise segments. Additional gentle walking can be done as a warm-up and warm down for 5-10 minutes

Week 1

Mission: You are just beginning, so don't push into pain or discomfort. Finish each session knowing that you could do more. For those who want to learn to run, run for 5-10 seconds, then walk for 1-2 minutes.

Mon	Tue	Wed	Thurs	Fri	Sat	Sun
Off	10 min	Off	12-14 min	Off	14-16 min	Off

Week 2

Mission: You are continuing to increase time and distance. On Sunday, pick a scenic place if you are walking or running. This week, beginning runners should run for 5-12 seconds, then walk 1-2 minutes.

Mon	Tue	Wed	Thurs	Fri	Sat	Sun
15-18 min	Off	17-19 min	Off	15 min	Off	19-21 min

Week 3

Mission: You're really making progress now—getting up near the half hour mark! On Saturday, ask some friends to go with you for the warm up and warm down—and have a picnic afterward. Some may join you. You've made it 3 weeks—keep going! You have an easy week coming. Beginning runners: the running segments can increase to 10-14 seconds of running, followed by 1-2 minutes of walking.

Mon	Tue	Wed	Thurs	Fri	Sat	Sun
Off	21-23 min	Off	23-25 min	Off	25-27 min	Off

Week 4

Mission: Rest a bit. This is an easier week, to make sure the body catches up. You have earned this. Beginning runners: run for the same run-walk ratio as in week 3.

Mon	Tue	Wed	Thurs	Fri	Sat	Sun
20-22 min	Off	20 min	Off	23 min	Off	25 min

You will do this! Just focus on each day, and make the little adjustments that you need to make. While you are doing your workouts, you can plan your success party. If you pick the right people, you may have some converts and companions who will join you in your mission and start exercising with you!

The Next 22 Weeks

"You've made it through the toughest part of the program, you only need to maintain momentum now."

This chapter is designed for those who've finished the program in the last chapter or who've been exercising for several weeks or months on their own. Continue to use 1-3 minute exercise segments, with 1-2 minutes of rest. But if you wish, you can extend the length of each segment to 3-5 min each, with 2-3 min of rest between each. Those who are beginning to run can follow the guidelines of run-walk-run as noted above each week. If the amount of exercise is too much for you (lingering fatigue, huffing and puffing, aches and pains, etc.) drop back to a ratio with more rest that feels comfortable. Continue to alternate the various segments of exercise in 2-3 minute segments, with a 1-2 minute walk between segments.

Training Program: Weeks 5-26

Week 5—run 10-14 seconds/walk 1-2 min (getting started runners)

Mon	Tue	Wed	Thurs	Fri	Sat	Sun
20 min	walk 22 min	20 min	walk 22 min	Off	25 min	walk 22 min

Week 6—-run 10-14 seconds/walk 1-2 min (getting started runners)

Mon	Tue	Wed	Thurs	Fri	Sat	Sun
22 min	walk 23 min	22 min	walk 23 min	Off	26 min	walk 25min

Week 7—run 10-14 seconds/walk 1-2 min (getting started runners) easy week to recover

Mon	Tue	Wed	Thurs	Fri	Sat	Sun
16 min	walk 18 min	16 min	walk 18 min	Off	20 min	walk 20min

Week 8—run 12-16 seconds/walk 1-2 min (getting started runners)

Mon	Tue	Wed	Thurs	Fri	Sat	Sun
24 min	walk 24 min	24 min	walk 24 min	Off	29 min	walk 28min

Week 9—run 12-16 seconds/walk 1-2 min (getting started runners)

Mon	Tue	Wed	Thurs	Fri	Sat	Sun
25 min	walk 25 min	25 min	walk 25 min	Off	32 min	walk 32 min

Week 10—run 12-16 seconds/walk 60-90 seconds (getting started runners) easy week

Mon	Tue	Wed	Thurs	Fri	Sat	Sun
20 min	walk 20 min	20 min	walk 20 min	Off	24 min	walk 25 min

Week 11—run 14-18 seconds/walk 60-90 sec (getting started runners)

Mon	Tue	Wed	Thurs	Fri	Sat	Sun
26 min	walk 26 min	26 min	walk 26 min	Off	34 min	walk 36 min

Week 12—run 14-18 seconds/walk 60-90 sec (getting started runners)

Mon	Tue	Wed	Thurs	Fri	Sat	Sun
27 min	walk 27 min	27 min	walk 27 min	Off	36 min	walk 40 min

Week 13—run 14-18 seconds/walk 55-90 sec (getting started runners) easy week

Mon	Tue	Wed	Thurs	Fri	Sat	Sun
20 min	walk 20 min	20 min	walk 20 min	Off	29 min	walk 30 min

Week 14—run 16-18 seconds/ walk 55-80 sec (getting started runners)

Mon	Tue	Wed	Thurs	Fri	Sat	Sun
28 min	walk 28 min	28 min	walk 28 min	Off	38 min	walk 44 min

Week 15—run 16-18 seconds/walk 50-80 sec (getting started runners)

Mon	Tue	Wed	Thurs	Fri	Sat	Sun
29 min	walk 29 min	29 min	walk 29 min	Off	40 min	walk 48 min

Week 16—run 16-18 seconds/walk 50-75 sec (getting started runners) easy week

Mon	Tue	Wed	Thurs	Fri	Sat	Sun
20 min	walk 20 min	22 min	walk 20 min	off	31 min	walk 35 min

Week 17—run 18-20 seconds/walk 45-75 sec (getting started runners)

Mon	Tue	Wed	Thurs	Fri	Sat	Sun
30 min	walk 30 min	30 min	walk 30 min	off	42 min	walk 52 min

Week 18—run 18-20 seconds/walk 45-70 sec (getting started runners)

Mon	Tue	Wed	Thurs	Fri	Sat	Sun
30 min	walk 30 min	30 min	walk 30 min	off	44 min	walk 56 min

Week 19—run 18-20 seconds/walk 40-70 sec (getting started runners) easy week

Mon	Tue	Wed	Thurs	Fri	Sat	Sun
20 min	walk 20 min	22 min	walk 20 min	off	33 min	walk 40 min

Week 20—run 20-22 seconds/walk 40-65 sec (getting started runners)

Mon	Tue	Wed	Thurs	Fri	Sat	Sun
30 min	walk 30 min	30 min	walk 30 min	off	46 min	walk 60 min

Week 21—run 20-22 seconds/walk 35-65 sec (getting started runners)

Mon	Tue	Wed	Thurs	Fri	Sat	Sun
30 min	walk 30 min	30 min	walk 30 min	off	48 min	walk 60 min

Week 22—run 20-22 seconds/walk 35-60 sec (getting started runners)

Mon	Tue	Wed	Thurs	Fri	Sat	Sun
22 min	walk 22 min	22 min	walk 22 min	off	35 min	walk 45 min

Week 23—run 22-24 seconds/walk 30-60 sec (getting started runners)

Mon	Tue	Wed	Thurs	Fri	Sat	Sun
30 min	walk 30 min	30 min	walk 30 min	off	50 min	walk 65 min

Week 24—run 22-24 seconds/walk 30-60 sec (getting started runners)

Mon	Tue	Wed	Thurs	Fri	Sat	Sun
30 min	walk 30 min	30 min	walk 30 min	off	52 min	walk 70 min

Week 25—run 22-24 seconds/walk 25-60 sec (getting started runners)

Mon	Tue	Wed	Thurs	Fri	Sat	Sun
22 min	walk 22 min	22 min	walk 22 min	off	37 min	walk 50 min

Week 26—run 24-26 seconds/ walk 25-60 sec (getting started runners)

Mon	Tue	Wed	Thurs	Fri	Sat	Sun
30 min	walk 30 min	30 min	walk 30 min	off	54 min	walk 70 min

Note: Continue after this point, alternating week # 25 and Week # 26.

How to Burn Up to 65 Pounds a Year

The long endurance workouts on the weekends will help to transform thousands of muscle cells into fat burning furnaces. By keeping the pace slow, and by inserting walk or shuffle breaks into every exercise session, you can avoid aches, pains and injuries. You'll also stay in the fat burning zone. A more gentle pace allows you to increase distance covered each week, significantly increasing the amount of calories burned.

10,000 or more steps a day (total of walking and running)
A pedometer, or step counter, can rev-up your fat burning. As you check your count, you have an incentive and reinforcement for adding extra steps to your day. It also gives you a sense of control over your actual calorie burn-off. During the first week, just count and record your daily amounts. During each week, for the next few weeks, try to increase the count by an additional 500 steps a day. Once you get into the goal of taking more than 10,000 steps a day in your everyday activities, you find yourself getting out of your chair more often, parking farther away from the supermarket, walking around the kid's playground, etc. In general, you learn how to move around instead of wait around. Each time you take a step, you burn fat.

These devices are usually about one inch square, and clip onto your belt, pocket or waistband. The simpler models just count steps and this is all you need. Other models compute miles and calories. I recommend getting one from a quality manufacturer. When tested, some of the really inexpensive ones registered 3-4 times as many steps as the quality products did—walking exactly the same course.

Your first goal is to gradually increase the daily step count to 10,000 by adding steps at home, at work, shopping, waiting for kids, etc., when you combine running and walking (or walking only). You will find many pockets of time during the day when you are just sitting or standing. When you "step around" instead of sit down, you burn fat and feel better. You become a more active and energetic person.

About dinnertime you should do a "step check". If you haven't acquired your 10,000, walk around the block a few extra times after dinner—or add to the total over the next few days. You don't have to stop with these figures. As you get into it, you'll find many more opportunities to walk….and burn. We regularly hear from women who initially had trouble getting in 5,000 steps. After 3 months they are exceeding 10,000, and a year later are averaging 15,000 with less weight on the body.

Up to 65 pounds of fat….gone during a year

Depending upon how many times you do the following each week, you have some significant opportunities for burning fat each day. These are easy movements that don't produce tiredness, aches or pains, but at the end of the year—it really adds up:

Lbs per year	Activity
1-2 pounds	taking the stairs instead of the elevator
2-14 pounds	getting out of your chair at work to walk down the hall
1-10 pounds	walking around instead of waiting: for a child, spouse, meeting, airplane, etc.
1-5 pounds	getting off the couch to move around the house (but not to get potato chips)
1-2 pounds	parking farther away from the supermarket, mall, church, etc.
1-3 pounds	parking farther away from your work
2-4 pounds	walking around the kids playground, practice field (chasing the kids)
2-4 pounds	walking up and down the concourse as you wait for your next flight
3-9 pounds	walking the dog each day

2-4 pounds	walking a couple of times around the block after supper
2-4 pounds	walking a couple of times around the block during lunch hour at work
2-4 pounds	walking an extra loop around the mall, supermarket, etc. to look for bargains (this last one could be expensive when at the mall)

Total: 20-65 pounds a year

Runners: 15 more pounds burned each year from adding a few extra miles a day
If you have time before and after your workout:

- Slow down and go one more mile on each run
- Walk a mile at lunchtime
- Jog a mile (walk 1.5-2 miles) before dinner, or afterward

Eating For Exercise

- Your muscles are the furnaces that move you forward and make you into a leaner person.

- They are the furnaces where fat is burned.

- They need a steady supply of fuel, vitamins, minerals, protein and other nutrients.

- Workouts train the muscle cells to increase capacity, performance and fat burning.

Warning: A radical change in the foods you eat is not a good idea, and usually leads to inadequate replenishment of key nutrients.

Mary needed more calories to burn more fat—60 pounds off still burning!

Mary works in a medical facility that spans several blocks. Two years ago, she hated having to go to a meeting across campus. Even at a slow pace, she huffed and puffed her way along—often struggling to keep up with the walking pace of two associates who weighed about 60 pounds less than she did. Recently, Mary walked with the same co-workers to the same location and led the way with no huffing and puffing. She felt like an athlete, with all of the positive mental boosts.

The decision that turned her around was joining the Albany, GA Galloway training group. Her target was a half marathon in six months. According to director Paula Bacon "Mary struggled with those early miles, but she never missed a Saturday training session. She had the most amazing sense of determination and you somehow knew that that there would be no stopping her".

"Since beginning this journey, my endurance and energy level is so much improved," Mary said. But one year after she began her training, the scales said that she had not lost any weight. So she made the fateful decision to seek guidance from a dietitian. Again, Mary was very "coachable" and carefully watched portion size, eating multiple times a day. She re-joined the half marathon training group.

At one point in the training, after losing many pounds, she reached a plateau. The dietitians found that she wasn't eating enough calories per day—and was probably reducing her daily step count due to low energy. With the addition of 200 more calories per day, she felt much better, and won 2nd place in her age group in a half marathon. Mary lost two pounds one week, three pounds another week—by restricting the intake and increasing the expenditure. She covers 15 miles every week as maintenance—more on the long training weekends. Mary also does strength training, elliptical and spinning on the days that she doesn't walk/run.

In this chapter, we will explain the nutrients that are most important, and can help in maintaining good overall health and fitness. If you want to make dietary changes, do so gradually.

As a regular exerciser you will not need significantly more vitamins and minerals, protein, etc. than a sedentary person. But if you don't get these ingredients for several days in a row, you will feel the effects when you try to exercise.

Most important nutrient: water

Whether you take in your fluids by drinking water, juice or other fluids, you should drink regularly throughout the day. Under normal circumstances, your thirst is a good guide for fluid consumption, but this is not the case among women over about 45 years old. Make sure that you have the equivalent of 6-8 glasses of various fluids each day, but if you are sweating a great deal, you will need to consume more. Alcoholic drinks are dehydrating: when having a glass of wine, add an additional glass of water. The fluid in caffeine beverages is only worth about half the fluid from water.

For reducing calorie intake, it's best to avoid drinks that have sugar or fat, in any form. Water is preferred because it has no calories and can help you feel more satisfied—especially when you've consumed one of your snacks or meals.

If you have to take bathroom stops during walks or workouts, you are probably drinking too much—either before or during the exercise. During an exertion session of 60 minutes or less, most exercisers don't need to drink at all. The intake of fluid before exercise should be arranged so that the excess fluid is eliminated before the start. Each person is a bit different, so you will have to find a routine that works for you. Very few individuals have to take bathroom breaks when stopping their fluid intake 2 hours before the start.

Hyponatremia—dangerous consumption of too much water

If you're exercising more than 4 hours at one time, and are drinking more than 27 oz of fluid per hour, you could be producing a dangerous depletion of sodium that may lead to death. Women are much more prone to this condition than men, possibly because they tend to drink more fluid for their body weight than men. Symptoms of this condition include the following, but none may be present:

- swelling of hands (to twice normal size)
- cramping in legs
- significant loss of concentration
- diarrhea or vomiting—if exercising for more than 4 hours and suffer from either, get help immediately.

Here's how to prevent this dangerous condition—when you are doing a long (4 hour +) workout:

- Drink less than 27 oz of fluid an hour.
- Avoid taking anti-inflammatory medication before or during an exercise session of more than 4 hours.
- Talk to your doctor about any medication you are taking— mentioning hyponatremia and that you plan to exercise more than 4 hours (if you plan to do so). Follow the doctor's advice concerning medication issues.
- If you cramp regularly, ask your doctor if you can take a salt tablet during exercise. (Succeed is a good one.)

Sweat the electrolytes

Electrolytes are the salts that your body loses when you sweat: sodium (primary), potassium (secondary but needed), magnesium and calcium (trace amounts needed each day). When these minerals get too low, your fluid transfer system doesn't work as well and you may experience ineffective cooling, swelling of the hands, and other problems. Most exercisers have no problem replacing these in a normal diet. But if you are experiencing leg muscle cramps during or after exercise, regularly, you may be low in sodium or potassium. The best product I've found for replacing these minerals is called SUCCEED. If you have high blood pressure, get your doctor's guidance before taking any salt supplement.

Practical eating issues

- You don't need to eat before exercise, unless your blood sugar is low (see the previous chapter).

- Reload most effectively by eating within 30 min of the finish of a workout (80% carb/20/protein).

- Eating or drinking too much right before the start will interfere with deep breathing, & may cause side pain. The food or fluid in your stomach limits your intake of air into the lower lungs and restricts the diaphragm.

- If you are running low on blood sugar at the end of your long workouts, take some blood sugar booster with you (see the previous chapter for suggestions).

- It is never a good idea to eat a huge meal. Those who claim that they must "carbo load" are usually rationalizing the desire to eat a lot of food. Eating a big meal the night before (or the day of) a long workout can be a real problem. You will have a lot of food in your gut, and you will be bouncing up and down for an extended period. Get the picture?

When you are sweating a lot, it is a good idea to drink several glasses a day (when not exercising) of a good electrolyte beverage. Accelerade, by Pacific Health Labs, is the best I've seen for both maintaining fluid levels and electrolyte levels.

Vitamins and Minerals

We strongly recommend a vitamin supplement, as a nutritional insurance policy. The best product we've found, based upon the research is Cooper Complete. This high quality product is designed and produced by Dr. Kenneth Cooper from Dallas Texas. There are several products for women at various stages of life. For more information, visit www.coopercomplete.com.

Calcium

The amount of calcium suggested for women who are approaching menopause or are experiencing menopause is 1500 mg per day. For most other women, the recommendation is 1000 mg a day. Be sure to read the section on women's issues about osteoporosis.

Iron

Pre-menopausal women tend to be low in iron. Exercise pushes the level even lower because the more you sweat, the more iron you lose. Cooking food in an iron skillet is an excellent way of acquiring iron that can be easily assimilated. Iron supplements are often hard to absorb, so check with your doctor if you are low in this nutrient. The best test is the serum ferritin test. Standard blood iron tests are not as effective in identifying low levels for exercisers. Post-menopausal women do not tend to have as many low iron issues, but monitor through your annual physical/blood work. If you are feeling tired for days at a time—especially during gentle workouts—it could be due to low iron levels.

What about Caffeine?

Research has shown that the consumption of the equivalent of a cup of coffee will extend endurance, and increase the fat burning potential. This central nervous system booster can rev up the body and mind, enhancing the quality and quantity of exercise each day/week. Unless you have heart rhythm problems, caffeine sensitivities, or other related problems, caffeine may enhance your exercise experience.

EXERCISE EATING SCHEDULE

- 1-2 hours before a morning workout: drink either a cup of coffee or a glass of water.
- Some exercisers feel better when they have an energy bar about 30-60 min before the workout.
- 30 min before, if blood sugar is low, take about100 calories of Accelerade or other blood sugar booster.
- Within 30 min after: take about 200 calories of an 80% carb/20% protein (Endurox R4, for example).
- If you are sweating a lot during hot weather, drink 3-4 glasses of a good electrolyte beverage like Accelerade throughout the day when not exercising.

Motivation

No More Excuses
How to Get Motivated and Stay Motivated

No More Excuses

All of us have days when we don't feel like exercising. Occasionally, you may need a day off, due to sickness, or too much physical activity. But usually this is not the case. Blame your excuses on the left side of your brain. When we are under stress in life (and who isn't) the left brain will have dozens of great reasons why we shouldn't work out. They are all perfectly logical and accurate. But we don't have to believe these messages. Once you quickly decide whether there is a medical reason for these blasts, you'll usually conclude that the left brain is just trying to make you lazy.

Thinking ahead and organizing your day will reduce or eliminate most of these excuses. You'll find pockets of time, more energy, quality time with kids and more enjoyment in the exertion. You'll tend to be more productive in everything you do because you have "your time to yourself".

The following is a list of excuses that most of us hear on a regular basis. With each, there's a strategy for blasting them away. Most of the time, it's as simple as just getting out there. Remember, you can be the captain of your ship. If you take charge over your schedule and your attitude, you will plan ahead, and you will get out and exercise. As you learn to ignore the left brain, and put one foot in front of the other, the endorphins start flowing, and the excuses start to melt away. Life is good!

"This _____ hurts!"

Most of us have several "weak links". These areas of the body are the first to hurt when we are stressed and talk to us more on the days when we have more stress. If there is no inflammation, loss of function, or real pain, it is usually OK to exercise. Indeed, exercise releases the stress which can erase or reduce the pains. But if you have any medical concerns, talk to a doctor who wants you to keep exercising.

It's a physiological fact that stress can greatly aggravate the symptoms of your weak links. Read more about this in MINDBODY PRESCRIPTION by Dr. John Sarno. While there is almost always some aggravation in an area, stress can reduce the blood supply and aggravate the nerve response, producing an increase in the intensity of the symptoms. Gentle exercise can bring blood flow to the area while it releases stress.

"I don't have time to exercise"

Most of the recent US Presidents have been regular exercisers, as well as most of their vice presidents. Are you busier than the President? You don't have to exercise for 30 minutes straight. You will get the same benefit from your weekday workouts by doing them in pockets of time: 5 minutes here, 10 minutes there. Many who start an exercise program find that they don't need as much sleep as they get in better shape, and exercise for 30 minutes or so before the day gets started. It all gets down to the question "Are you going to take control over the organization of your day or not?" Spend a few minutes in the morning to arrange your schedule. By making time for exercise, you'll also tend to be more productive and efficient, and will "pay back" the time you spend. Bottom line is that you have the time—seize it and you will have more quality in your life. Your loved ones will appreciate this too, because after a workout, you're nicer to them.

TIP: CRAMPED FOR TIME? JUST WALK FOR 5 MINUTES

The main reason that beginners don't make progress is that they don't exercise regularly. Whatever it takes to keep you going every other day—do it. Even if you only have 5-10 minutes, you will maintain most of the adaptations. Besides, if you start with the idea of going for 5 minutes, you'll usually stay out for 10 or 15.

"People will talk about me"

Many women deprive themselves of the fat burning, the vitality enhancement and the attitude boost of walking because they are afraid that someone driving by will see them exercising, and judge them in some way. Actually, most people admire and respect those who spend the energy to exercise—whether they look like athletes or not. Besides, it's not a good idea to let the opinions of unknown people stop you from doing something that can enhance your life.

Exercise makes me tired

If this happens, you are the one responsible. You have almost complete control over this situation. By starting each walk with a good blood sugar level, paced conservatively, with sufficient "shuffle" breaks, then you will feel better and more energized than before you started. If you have a bad habit of going too fast in the beginning, then get control over yourself! As you learn to slow down, you'll go farther and have more energy at the end—and afterwards.

I don't have the right build (or technique) for exercise

Just go to any large gym and you'll see an amazing diversity of body types—including those who weigh more than 300 pounds. Virtually every one of us is genetically designed to walk, and when we do so regularly, our movements become more and more efficient and natural. Even if you don't have smooth form, you can enjoy the way you feel during and afterward. With all of the different pieces of equipment, you can find one that will work for you.

I need to spend some time with my kids

There are a number of exercise strollers that allow parents to walk with their kids. The two of us logged thousands of miles with our first child, Brennan, in single "baby jogger". We got a twin carrier after Westin was born. With the right pacing, you can talk to the kids about anything, and they can't run or crawl away.

You can also walk around a playground as you watch them play, or walk around a track while they play on the infield. Home equipment allows busy moms and dads to get in their workout as they watch kids napping or watching TV, or talk with them while they are playing.

I've got too much work to do

There will always be work to do. Several surveys have found that exercisers get more work done on days they work out. Walking (when paced correctly) can leave you with more energy and a better attitude while you prepare to manage your day. All of this comes with an erasure of stress. Hundreds of morning exercisers have told me that during the quiet morning exercise, they plan their day and solve problems. Others say that the after-work "workout" relieved stress, tied up some of the mental loose ends from the office, and allowed for a transition to home life. You will get as much (probably more) work done each day if you work out regularly.

I don't have the energy to exercise today

This is one of the easier ones to solve. Most of the exercisers who've consulted us about this excuse had not been eating enough times a day. We don't mean eating more food. In most cases, the quantity of food is reduced. By eating about every 2-3 hours, most feel more energized, more of the time. Even if you aren't eating well during the day, you can overcome low blood sugar by having a "booster" snack about an hour before a workout. Caffeine, taken about an hour before exercise, helps (as long as you don't have caffeine sensitivities). The dynamic food duo that we use is an energy bar and a cup of coffee. Just carry some convenient food with you at all times.

I don't have my walking shoes and clothes with me

Load an old bag or backpack with a pair of running shoes, a top for both winter and summer, shorts and warm-up pants, towel, deodorant, and anything else you would need for exercise and clean up. Put the bag next to the front door, or in the trunk of your car, etc. Then, the next time you are waiting to pick up your child from soccer, etc., you can do a quick change in the restroom and make some loops around the field, school, etc.

How to Get Motivated and Stay Motivated

- Consistency is the most important part of conditioning and fitness.
- Motivation is the most important factor in being consistent.
- You can gain control over your motivation—everyday.

The choice is yours. You can take control over your attitude, or you can let yourself be swayed by outside factors that will leave you on a motivational roller coaster: fired up one day, and down the next. Getting motivated on a given day can sometimes be as simple as *saying* a few key words and getting out the door. But staying motivated requires a strategy or motivational training program. To understand the process, we must first look inside your head.

Think of the brain as having two major communication circuits: a logical circuit and a creative and gutteral one. The logical side (often called the "left brain") does our business activities, trying to steer us into pleasure and away from discomfort. The creative and intuitive center (commonly the "right brain") has the capacity to solve an unlimited number of problems as it connects us to hidden strengths.

As we accumulate stress, the left brain sends us a stream of logical messages telling us "you don't need to exercise today," or, "you've got so much to do," or, "this isn't your day," and even philosophical messages like, "why are you doing this?" We are all capable of staying on track, and maintaining motivation even when the left brain tries to stop us. Take command over motivation by ignoring the left brain unless there is a legitimate reason of health or safety (very rare). You can deal with the left brain, through a series of mental training drills.

The following drills prepare the right side of the brain to work on solutions to the problems you are having. As the negative messages spew out of the left brain, the right brain doesn't argue—it just goes to work. By preparing mentally for the challenges you expect, you will empower the right brain to find solutions and develop mental toughness. But even more important, you will gain confidence from just having a strategy comprised of proven ways to deal with the problems.

Rehearsing Success

#1 Getting out the door after a hard day

By rehearsing yourself through a motivation problem, you can be more consistent and set yourself up for improvement. You must first have a goal that is do-able, and a rehearsal situation that is realistic. Let's learn by doing:

1. State your desired outcome: To get in a long walk after a hard day at work.

2. Detail the challenge: Low blood sugar and fatigue, a stream of negative messages, need to get the evening meal ready to be cooked, overwhelming desire to feel relaxed.

3. Break up the challenge into a series of actions, which lead you through the mental barriers, no one of which is challenging to the left brain.

- You're driving home at the end of the day, knowing that it is a scheduled exercise day but you have no energy.
- Your left brain says: "You're too tired." "Take the day off." "You don't have the energy to exercise."
- So you say to the left brain: "I'm not going to exercise. I'll put on some comfortable shoes and clothes, eat and drink, get food preparation going for dinner and feel relaxed.

- You're in your room, putting on comfortable clothes and shoes (they just happen to be used for walking).
- You're drinking coffee (tea, diet cola, etc.) and eating a good tasting energy snack, as you get the food prepared to go into the oven.
- Stepping outside, you check on the weather.
- You're walking to the edge of your block to see what the neighbors are doing.
- As you cross the street, you're on your way.
- The endorphins are kicking in, you feel good, you want to continue.

Lesson: A body on the couch wants to remain there. But once a body gets in motion, it wants to stay in motion.

4. Rehearse the situation over and over, fine-tuning it so that it becomes integrated into the challenges of your life and is in "sync" with the way you think and act.

5. Enjoy the reward. Finish by mentally focusing on the good feelings experienced with the desired outcome. You have felt the good attitude, the vitality, the glow from a good walk, and you are truly relaxed. So revisit these positive feelings at the end of each rehearsal.

#2 Getting your home gym workout going, early in the morning

The second most common motivational problem that we're asked about relates to the comfort of the bed, upon waking, when it's time for exercise.

1. State your desired outcome: To get my workout in before work

2. Detail the challenge: Desire to lie in bed, no desire to exert yourself so early. The stress of the alarm clock, and having to think about what to do next when the brain isn't working very fast.

3. Break up the challenge into a series of actions, which lead you through the mental barriers, no one of which is challenging to the left brain.

- The night before, lay out your exercise clothes and shoes, near your coffee pot, so that you don't have to think.
- Set your alarm, and say to yourself over and over: alarm off, feet on the floor, to the coffee pot or "alarm, floor, coffee." As you repeat this, you visualize doing each action without thinking. By repeating it, you lull yourself to sleep. You have also been programming yourself for taking action the next morning.
- The alarm goes off. You shut it off, put feet on the floor, and you head to the coffee pot—all without thinking.
- You're putting on one piece of clothing at a time, sipping coffee, without thinking about exercise.
- With coffee cup in hand, walk into the home gym.
- Sipping coffee, you walk around the equipment.
- Putting coffee down, you work out on one piece of equipment for 2 minutes. You're on your way!
- The endorphins are kicking in, you feel good, you want to continue.

Lesson: A body on the bed wants to stay on the bed. But once that body gets moving, it wants to keep moving.

Rehearsals lead to patterns of behavior more easily if you don't think—but just move from one action to the next. The power of the rehearsal is that you have formatted your brain for a series of actions so that you move from one to the next. As you repeat the pattern, revising it for real life, you become what you want to be. You are successful!

Tips & Techniques

The Correct Shoe Can Make a Huge Difference
Walking Form and Shuffling
The Galloway Run-Walk-Run™ Method
Staying Injury Free

The Correct Shoe Can Make a Huge Difference

"I couldn't believe the difference in my running when I found a shoe designed for my feet."

Ask several runners or walkers, particularly those who have exercised for 10 years or more about the running stores in your area. Pick a store that has a reputation for spending time with each customer to find a shoe that will best match the shape and function of the foot. Be prepared to spend at least 45 minutes in the store. Quality stores are often busy, and quality fitting takes time. Getting good advice can save your feet. Experienced and committed running shoe staff members match you up with shoes through a complex series of observations of your feet and legs, based upon experience. We hear from exercisers about every week, who purchased a "great deal" but had to use it for lawn mowing because it wasn't designed for the way their feet moved during exercise.

Bring your most worn pair of shoes you own —walking or running

The pattern of wear on a well-used walking or running shoe reveals the way your foot functions, as "read" by a shoe expert.

A knowledgeable shoe store staff person can usually notice how your foot functions

…by watching you walk and run. This is a skill gained through the experience of fitting thousands of feet.

Give feedback

As you work with the person in the store you need to give feedback as to how the shoe fits and feels. You want the shoe to protect your foot while usually allowing the foot to go through a running/walking motion that is natural for you. Tell the staff person what activities you will be doing and if there are pressure points or pains—or that it just doesn't feel right.

Reveal any injuries or foot problems

If you have had shin pain, or some joint issues (knee, hip, ankle) possibly caused by the "overpronation" of your foot (foot rolls to the inside as it pushes off) you may need a shoe that protects your foot from this excess motion. Try several shoes in the "stability" category to see which seems to feel best. If you need more support, you'll move to the "motion control" group.

Don't try to fix your foot if it isn't broken

Even if your foot rolls excessively one way or the other, you don't necessarily need to get an over-controlling shoe. Your feet and legs make many adjustments and adaptations which keep many exercisers injury free—even when they have extreme motions that are harmful to others.

Expensive shoes are often not the best for you

The most expensive shoes are usually not the best shoes for most feet. You cannot assume that high price will buy you extra protection from injury or more miles. At the price of some of the shoes, you might expect that they would do the exercise for you. They won't.

Go by fit and not the size noted on the box of the shoe

Most women will fit best into a sports shoe that is about 1-2 sizes larger than their street shoe. Be open to getting the best fit—regardless of what size you see on the running shoe box. Shoe experts can guide you here, also.

Extra room for your toes—about half an inch

Your foot tends to swell during the day, so it's best to fit your shoes after noontime. Be sure to stand up in the shoe during the fitting process to measure how much extra room you have in the toe region of the shoe. Pay attention to the length of your feet, and leave at least half an inch.

Width issues

- Running/walking shoes tend to be a bit wider than street shoes.
- Usually, the lacing can "snug up" the difference, if your foot is a bit narrower.
- The shoe shouldn't be laced too tight around your foot because the foot swells during exercise. On hot days, the average foot will swell one-half to a full shoe size.
- In general, running shoes are designed to handle a certain amount of "looseness". But if you are getting blisters when wearing a loose shoe, snug the laces.
- Several shoe companies have some shoes in varying widths.

Shoes for women

Women's shoes tend to be slightly narrower than those for men, and the heel is usually a bit smaller. The quality of the women's versions of major running shoe brands is equal to those of men. But about 25% of women exercisers have feet that can fit better into men's shoes. Usually the confusion comes among women who wear large sizes. Staff members in the better running stores can help you make a choice in this area.

If the shoe color doesn't match your outfit, it's not the end of the world

I receive several emails every year concerning injuries that were produced by wearing the wrong shoe. Some of these are "fashion injuries" in which the runner picked a shoe only because the color matched the new outfit. Remember that there are no fashion police out there on the sidewalks or trails or gyms.

BREAKING IN A NEW SHOE

- Wear the new shoe around the house, for a few minutes each day for a week. If you stay on carpet, and the shoe doesn't fit correctly, you can exchange it at the store. But if you have put some wear (dirt, etc.) on the shoe, few stores will take it back.

- In most cases you will find that the shoe feels comfortable enough to exercise immediately, but this is not a good idea. It is best to continue walking in the shoe, gradually allowing the foot to accommodate to the inner shoe construction: arch, heel area, ankle pads, and to make other adjustments. If you exercise in the shoe too soon, blisters are often the result.

- If there are no rubbing issues on the foot when walking, you could walk in the new shoe for a gradually increasing amount for 2-4 days.

- On the first exercise session in the new shoe, use the shoe for 4-5 minutes. Then, put on your old shoes and continue.

- On each successive workout, increase the amount done in the new shoe for 3-4 sessions. At this point, you will usually have the new shoe broken in.

HOW DO YOU KNOW WHEN IT'S TIME TO GET A NEW SHOE?

- When you have been using a shoe for 3-4 weeks successfully, buy another pair of exactly the same model, make, size, etc. The reason for this: The shoe companies often make significant changes or discontinue shoe models (even successful ones) every 6-8 months.

- Gradually break in the new pair as noted above.

- After the shoe feels broken in, on one of your weekly workouts use the new shoe for a few minutes, then shift to the shoe that is already broken in.

- On the "shoe break-in" day, gradually exercise a little more in the new shoe. Continue to do this only one day a week. Be sure to shift back to your old shoe for a comparison.

- Several weeks later you will notice that the new shoe offers more bounce than the old one.

- When the old shoe doesn't offer the support you like, shift to the new pair. Don't wait until the old pair is "shot".

- Start breaking in a third pair.

Note: There's more information on shoes and fitting in Galloway's Book on Running, Second Edition, and in most of my other books, listed at the end of this book.

Walking Form and "Shuffling"

Most people walk correctly when they use a gentle and comfortable walking motion. But every year, there are walkers who get injured because they are walking in a way that aggravates some area of the foot or leg. Most of these problems come from trying to walk too fast, with too long a stride, or from using a race walk or power walk technique (which I don't recommend).

1. *Avoid a long walking stride.* Maintain a relaxed motion that does not stress the knees, tendons or muscles of the leg, feet, knees or hips. If you feel pain or aggravation in these areas, shorten stride. Many walkers find that they can walk fairly fast with a short stride. When in doubt, walk more slowly and gently.

2. ***Don't lead with your arms.*** Minimal arm swing is best. Swinging the arms too much can encourage a longer walk stride which can result in aches and pains. The extra rotation of knees, hips, etc., can lead to longer recovery or injury. The legs should set the rhythm for your walk, allowing you to get into a delightful pattern of right brain thoughts that some call "the zone".

3. ***Let your feet move in the way that is natural for them***. When walkers try unnatural techniques that supposedly increase stride length by landing further back on the heel or pushing further on the toe than the legs are designed to move, many get injured. I don't recommend race walking or power walking for this reason.

4. ***Walking sticks?*** Many long distance walkers have enjoyed using this European import, which gives the hands and arms "something to do". These adapted ski poles have hand grips that are molded to the human hand for secure gripping. On tough terrain, they may aid in balance. On flat terrain the poles lightly touch the ground. When pesky dogs appear, you have a means of defense. In races, however, they may trip up other walkers or runners.

"Shuffling" can reduce fatigue, soreness, aches

"Shuffling is barely moving your feet and legs, to let the walking muscles recover"

Most of the time you're doing it right if you feel comfortable, aren't huffing and puffing, and don't have any aches or pains after your first 10 minutes of walking. You are the captain of your walking ship and it is you who determines how far, how fast, how much you will walk, etc. If you choose to insert shuffle breaks from the beginning of any walk that is long for you, you will reduce fatigue, aches and pains.

What is a "shuffle"?

With your feet next to the ground, use a short stride with minimal movement. You're still moving forward, but not having to spend much energy doing so. When you insert 30-60 seconds of shuffling into a regular walk, every 2-4 minutes, your walking muscles relax and rest. This lowers the chance of aches and pains due to the constant use of the muscles, tendons, etc.

Shuffle before you get tired
Most of us, even when untrained, can walk for several miles before fatigue sets in, because walking is an activity that we are designed to do for hours. Many beginners get discouraged, however, because during the first session or two they don't feel that they are going as far as they should—and add a mile or two. During the extra mileage they often feel strong, and hardly tired. In a day or two they know otherwise as overused muscles complain.

The continuous use of the walking muscles and tendons—even when the walking pace feels completely comfortable—increases stress on our "weak links", increasing aches, and pains much more quickly. If you shuffle before your walking muscles start to get tired, you recover instantly. This increases your capacity for exercise while reducing the chance of a next-day soreness attack.

A strategy that gives you control
You can't wait until you're tired—you must insert the "shuffles" from the beginning. In setting up a conservative strategy of walk/shuffle, you gain control over fatigue, soreness, and aches. Using this fatigue-reduction tool early gives you muscle strength and mental confidence to the end. Even when you don't need the extra muscle strength and resiliency bestowed by the method, you will feel better during and after your walk, and will finish knowing that you could have gone further, while recovering faster.

A short and very gentle shuffle
During the shuffle you are only slightly moving your feet and legs. This allows the tendons, muscles, etc. to recover from your regular walking motion. Keep the feet next to the ground, taking baby steps, barely moving the legs.

No need to ever eliminate the shuffle breaks

Some beginners assume that they must work toward the day when they don't have to take any shuffle breaks at all. This is up to the individual, but is not recommended. Remember that you decide what ratio of walk-shuffle to use. I suggest that you adjust the ratio to how you feel on a given day.

Even the most experienced walker has a few "weak links" that are irritated from continuous use. Shuffling can manage these— or eliminate them.

How to keep track of the shuffle breaks

There are several watches which can be set to beep when it's time to shuffle, and then beep again when it's time to walk. Check my website (www.jeffgalloway.com) or a good running store for advice in this area.

How to use shuffle breaks

1. Beginners could walk for 2 minutes and shuffle for 30 seconds. If you feel good during and after the walk, continue with this ratio. If not, adjust the ratio until you feel good.

2. Shuffle breaks allow the body to warm up more easily. If your legs feel tight or you have some soreness, walk for a minute and shuffle for 20-30 seconds—for the first 10 minutes. As the legs loosen up, reduce the shuffles as necessary.

3. On walks longer than about 45 minutes, even experienced walkers find that a 30 second shuffle, after about 4 min of walking, helps recovery, and reduces aches and pains.

4. On any given day, when you need more shuffling, do so. Don't ever be afraid to drop back to make the walk more fun, and less tiring.

The Galloway Run-Walk-Run™ Method

"The scheduled use of walk breaks, gives each runner control over fatigue and running enjoyment."

One of the wonderful aspects of running is that there is no definition of a "runner" that you must live up to. There are also no rules that you must follow as you do your daily run. You are the captain of your running ship and it is you who determines how far, how fast, how much you will run, walk, etc. While you will hear many opinions on this, running has always been a freestyle type of activity where each individual is empowered to mix and match the many variables and come out with the running experience that he or she chooses. Walking is the most important component for the first time runner, and can even give the veteran a chance to improve time. Here's how it works.

Walk before you get tired

Most of us, even when untrained, can walk for several miles before fatigue sets in, because walking is an activity that we are bio-engineered to do for hours. Running is more work, because you have to lift your body off the ground and then absorb the shock of the landing, over and over. This is why the continuous use of the running muscles will produce fatigue, aches, and pains much more quickly. If you insert a walk break into a run before your running muscles start to get tired, you allow the muscle to recover instantly—increasing your capacity for exercise while reducing the chance of next-day soreness.

The "method" part involves having a strategy. By using a ratio of running and walking, listed below, you will manage your fatigue. Using this fatigue-reduction tool early will save muscle resources and bestow the mental confidence to cope with any challenges that may come later. Even when you don't need the extra muscle strength and resiliency bestowed by the method, you will feel better during and after your run, and finish knowing that you could have gone further.

You will be primarily walking at first. By inserting short segments of running, followed by longer walk breaks, your muscles adapt to running, without getting overwhelmed. As you improve your running ability, you will reach a point where you can set the ratio of running and walking—for that day.

"The run-walk method is very simple: you run for a short segment and then take a walk break, and keep repeating this pattern."

Walk breaks allow you to take control over fatigue, in advance, so that you can enjoy every run. By taking them early and often you can feel strong, even after a run that is very long for you. Beginners will alternate very short run segments with short walks. Even elite runners find that walk breaks on long runs allow them to recover faster. There is no need to reach the end of a run, feeling exhausted—if you insert enough walk breaks, for you, on that day.

Walk Breaks....

- Give you control over your level of fatigue
- erase fatigue
- push back your tiredness "wall"
- allow for endorphins to collect during each walk break—you feel good!
- break up the distance into manageable units. ("one more minute until a walk break")
- speed recovery
- reduce the chance of aches, pains and injury
- allow you to feel good afterward—doing what you need to do without debilitating fatigue
- give you all of the endurance of the distance of each session—without the pain
- allow older runners to recover fast, and feel as good or better than the younger days

A short and gentle walking stride

It's better to walk slowly, with a short stride. There has been some irritation of the shins, when runners or walkers maintain a stride that is too long.

No need to ever eliminate the walk breaks

Some beginners assume that they must work toward the day when they don't have to take any walk breaks at all. This is up to the individual, but is not recommended. Remember that you decide what ratio of run-walk-run to use. There is no rule that requires you to run any ratio of run-walk on any given day. I suggest that you adjust the ratio to how you feel.

I've run for about 50 years, and enjoy running more than ever because of walk breaks. Each run I take energizes my day. I would not be able to run almost every day if I didn't insert the walk breaks early and often. I start most runs taking a short walk break every minute.

How to keep track of the walk breaks

There are several watches which can be set to beep when it's time to walk, and then beep again when it's time to start up again. Check our website (www.jeffgalloway.com) or a good running store for advice in this area.

How to use breaks

1. Start by running for 5-10 seconds, and walking 1-2 minutes.
2. If you feel good during and after the run, continue with this ratio. If not, run less until you feel good.
3. After 3-6 sessions at the ratio, add 5-10 seconds of running, maintaining the same amount of walking.
4. When you can run for 30 seconds, gradually reduce the walking time to 30 seconds, every 3-6 sessions.
5. When 30 seconds/30 seconds feels too easy, gradually increase the running time, 5-10 sec every 3-6 sessions.
6. On any given day, when you need more walking, do it. Don't ever be afraid to drop back to make the run more fun, and less tiring.

Staying Injury Free

Because running and walking are activities that enabled our ancient ancestors to survive, we have the ability to adapt to these two patterns of motion if we use these principles:

- Walk or run at a gentle pace—and insert shuffle breaks/walk breaks from the beginning.
- Schedule sufficient rest between each workout.
- Exercise regularly—about every other day.
- When we increase exercise, do so very gradually, and reduce the intensity of the longer workout.
- The single greatest reason for improvement in walking or running is *not getting injured.*

But inside each human is a personality trait that can compromise exercise enjoyment. I call this the "Type A overworker syndrome". Even those who feel they have no competitive urges and no athletic background need to be on guard. Once a new exerciser has achieved a certain level of fitness, there is a tendency to push more or rest less. At first, the body responds. When the exerciser keeps pushing, the body breaks at one of the "weak links". Here are some guidelines given as one exerciser to another.

Be sensitive to weak links

Each of us has a very few areas that take on more stress, and tend to register most of the aches, pains and injuries. The most common sites are the knees, the foot, the shins and the hip. Those who have been exercising for a year or more will usually know their own weak links. If you have a particular place on your knee that has been hurt before, and it hurts during or after exercise, take an extra day or two off, and follow the suggestions concerning treating an injury, listed below.

How do you know that you are injured?

The following are the leading signs that you have an injury. If you feel any of the three below, you should stop your workout immediately and take some extra rest days (at least 2 days). Continuing to do the same exercise that irritated the tendon, muscle, etc., at the early stages of an injury, creates a dramatically worse injury—even during one workout. If you take 2-3 days off at the first symptom, you may avoid having to stop exercise for 2-3 months by trying to push through the pain. It is always safer to err on the side of taking more time off when you first notice one of the following:

1. *Inflammation*—any type of swelling

2. *Loss of function*—the knee, foot, etc., doesn't work correctly

3. *Pain*—that does not go away when you walk for a few minutes

Losing conditioning

Studies have shown that you can maintain conditioning even when you don't exercise for 5 days. Surely you want to continue regular exercise if you can, but staying injury free has an even higher priority. So don't be afraid to take up to 5 days off when a "weak link" kicks in. In most cases you will only stop for 2-3 days.

Treatment

It is always best, at the first sign of a real injury, to see a doctor (or with muscle injury—a massage therapist) who wants to get you exercising again as soon as possible. The better doctors will explain what they believe is wrong (or tell you when he/she cannot come up with a diagnosis) and give you a treatment plan. This will give you great confidence in the process, which has been shown to speed the healing.

Treatments while you are waiting to see a doctor.

Unfortunately, most of the better doctors are so booked up that it may take several days and sometime weeks to see them. While waiting for your appointment, here are some things other exercisers have done when one of the weak links kick in:

1. Take 2-5 days off from any activity that could irritate it.
2. If the area is next to the skin (tendon, foot, etc.), rub a chunk of ice on the area(s)—constantly rubbing for 15 min until the area gets numb. Continue to do this for a week after you feel no symptoms. The chunk of ice must be rubbed constantly and directly on the tissue where the injury is located. (Ice bags and gel ice do virtually nothing.)
3. If the problem is inside a joint or muscle, call your doctor and ask if you can use prescription strength anti-inflammatory medication. Don't take any medication without a doctor's advice—and follow that advice.
4. If you have a muscle injury, see a very successful sports massage therapist. Find one who has a lot of successful experience treating the area where you are injured. The magic fingers and hands can often work wonders.

Preventing injury

Having had over a hundred injuries myself, and then having worked with tens of thousands who have worked through aches and pains, I've developed the suggestions below. They are based upon my experience and are offered as one exerciser to another. I'm proud to report that since I started following the advice that I give others, I've not had an overuse injury in over 30 years.

Take 48 hours between strenuous workouts
Exercising longer or faster (for you), puts a lot more stress on the muscles, tendons, etc. Allowing tired muscles to rest for two days can work magic in recovery. Stair machine work should also be avoided during the 48 hour rest period (stair work uses the same muscles as running and strenuous walking). Also avoid any other activities that seem to irritate the aggravated area.

Don't stretch!
I've come full circle on this. A high percentage of the exercisers who report to me, injured, have either become injured because

they stretched or aggravated the injury by stretching. When they stop stretching, most have reported that the injury starts healing, in a relatively short period of time. The exception to this rule is in the treatment of Iliotibial band injury. For this injury alone, stretching the I-T band seems to help walkers continue to exercise, while healing.

Do the "toe squincher" exercise
(prevention of foot and heel injuries)
This exercise can be done 10-30 times a day, on both feet (one at a time). Point the toes and squinch them until the foot cramps (only a few seconds). This strengthens the many little muscles in the foot that can provide a platform of support. It is particularly effective in preventing plantar fascia.

Don't increase total mileage or minutes more than 10% a week

Monitor your quantity of exercise with a log book or calendar. If you exceed the 10 percent increase rule, take an extra day off.

Drop total mileage in half, every 3rd or 4th week —even when increasing by no more than 10% per week

Your log book can guide you here also. You won't lose any conditioning and you'll help the body heal itself and get stronger. A steady increase, week after week, does not allow the legs to catch up and rebuild.

Avoid a long stride—whether walking or running

Use more of a shuffle motion (feet close to the ground), and you'll reduce the chance of many injuries.

Troubleshooting

- How Do I Start Back when I've Had Time Off?
- It Hurts!
- No Energy Today
- Side Pain
- I Feel Great One Day—but not the Next
- No Motivation
- Cramps in my Leg Muscles
- Nausea or Diarrhea
- Headache
- Should I Exercise when I Have a Cold?
- Street Safety
- Dogs

How Do I Start Back, when I've Had Time Off?

The longer you've been away from exercise, the more gentle should be your increase during the return. I want to warn you that most exercisers reach a point during their "comeback" when they feel totally back in shape—and push too hard. Stay with the plan below for your return and when in doubt, be more conservative. Remember that you are in this for the long run! If you have any excess fatigue, aches or pains, drop back to a lower level of exercise.

Less than 2 weeks off You will feel like you are starting over again, but should come back quickly. Let's say that you were at week # 25 on the training program in this book but had to take 10 days off. Start back at week #2 for the first week. If all is well, skip to week # 4 for the second week. If that works well, gradually transition back to the schedule you were using before you had your layoff, over the next 2-3 weeks.

14 days to 29 days off You will also feel like you are starting over again, and it will take longer to get it all back: Within about 5-6 weeks you should be back to normal. Start with week # 1 and then week # 2. If there are no aches, pains or lingering fatigue, then use the schedule but skip every other week. After the 5th week, transition back into what you were doing before the layoff.

One month or more off If you have not exercised for a month or more, start over again, like a beginner. Use the schedule in this book, following it exactly (from week # 1) for the first few weeks. After 2-3 weeks, the safest plan is to continue with the schedule. But if you're having no aches and pains, and no lingering fatigue, you could increase more rapidly by skipping one week out of three. After 3 months of no problems, your conditioning may be back to the former level.

It Hurts! Is it just a Passing Ache, or a Real Injury?

Most of the aches and pains you feel when exercising will go away within a minute or two. If there is pain, stop the current exercise and walk around for 2-3 minutes. Then, try the exercise again, gently. If the pain comes back after doing this 4 or 5 times, try another exercise. Gentle walking will usually allow you to burn calories without incurring damage.

Walking pain When the pain stays around when walking, try a very short stride. Walk for a 30-60 seconds. If it still hurts when walking, try sitting down, and massaging the area that hurts, if you can. Sit for 2-4 minutes. When you try again to walk, and it still hurts, call it a day—your workout is over.

It's an injury if....

There's inflammation—swelling in the area
There's loss of function—the foot, knee, etc. doesn't work correctly
There's pain—it hurts and keeps hurting or gets worse
Treatment suggestions:

1. See a doctor who has treated other exercisers very successfully and wants to get you back working out.
2. Take at least 2-5 days off from any activity that could irritate it to get the healing started, more if needed.
3. If the area is next to the skin (tendon, foot, etc.), rub a chunk of ice on the area(s) constantly rubbing for 15 min until the area gets numb. Continue to do this for a week after you feel no symptoms. Ice bags and gel ice do no good at all in most cases.
4. If the problem is inside a joint or muscle, call your doctor and ask if you can use prescription strength anti-inflammatory medication for 2-3 days. Don't take any medication without a doctor's advice—and follow that advice.
5. If you have a muscle injury, see a veteran sports massage therapist. Try to find one who has a lot of successful experience treating the area where you are injured. The magic fingers and hands can often work wonders.

This is advice from one exerciser to another. For more info on injuries, treatment, etc. see a doctor and read the "Staying Injury Free" chapter in this book, and Galloway's Book on Running, Second Edition.

No Energy Today

There will be a number of days each year when you will not feel like exercising. On most of these, you can turn it around and feel great. Occasionally, you will not be able to do this, because of an infection, lingering fatigue, or other physical problems. Here's a list of things that can give you energy. If these actions don't lead you to a workout, then read the nutrition sections—particularly the blood sugar chapter in this book—or consult Galloway's Book on Running, Second Edition.

1. Eat an energy bar, with water or a caffeinated beverage, about an hour before the exercise. Caffeine helps!

2. Instead of #1, half an hour before exercising, you could drink 100-200 calories of a sports drink that has a mix of 80% simple carbohydrate and 20% protein. The product Accelerade has this already put together.

3. Just walk for 5 minutes away from your house, office, etc., and the energy often kicks in. Forward movement gets the attitude moving too.

4. One of the prime reasons for no energy, is that you didn't re-load within 30 minutes after your last exercise session. Next time consume 100-200 calories of a mix that is 80% simple carbohydrate and 20% protein (Endurox R4 is the product that has this formulated).

5. Low-carb diets will result in low energy to get motivated before a workout, and often less energy to finish the workout.

6. In most cases it is fine to keep going even if you aren't energetic. But if you sense an infection, see a doctor. If the low energy stays around for several days, see a nutritionist that knows about the special needs of exercisers and/or get some blood work done. This may be due to inadequate iron, B vitamins, energy stores, etc.

Note: If you have any problems with caffeine, don't consume any products containing it. As always, if you sense any health problem, see a doctor.

Side Pain

This is very common, and usually has a simple fix. Normally it is not anything to worry about...it just hurts. I believe that this condition is due to 1) the lack of lower lung breathing, and 2) Pushing the pace from the beginning of the workout. You can correct #2 easily by warming up more slowly at the beginning, and slowing down your workout pace—or reducing the duration of the segments.

Lower lung breathing from the beginning of a workout can prevent most side pain. This way of inhaling air is performed by diverting the air you breathe into your lower lungs. Also called "belly breathing" this is how we breathe when asleep, and it provides maximum opportunity for oxygen absorption. If you don't breathe this way when you work out, and you are not getting the oxygen you need, the side pain will tell you. By slowing down, and breathing deeply for a while, the pain may go away. But sometimes it does not. Most exercisers just continue with the side pain. In 50 years of running and helping others, I've not seen any lasting negative effect from those who run with a side pain.

You don't have to take in a maximum breath to perform this technique. Simply breathe a normal breath but send it to the lower lungs. You know that you have done this if your stomach goes up and down as you inhale and exhale. If your chest goes up and down, you are breathing shallowly.

Note: Never breathe in and out rapidly. This can lead to hyperventilation, dizziness, and fainting.

I Feel Great One Day...but not the Next

If you can solve this problem, you could become a very wealthy person. There are a few common reasons for this, but there will always be "those days" when the body doesn't seem to work right—the gravity seems heavier than normal—and you cannot find a reason.

1. Pushing through. In most cases, this is a one-day occurrence. Most runners just put more walking into the mix, and get through it. Those who do other exercises take a longer time to warm up or put more rest between segments. Before pushing, however, make sure that there is not a medical reason as a cause. Don't exercise when you have a lung infection, for example.

2. Heat and/or humidity will make you feel worse. You will often feel great when the temperature is below 60° F and miserable when 80° F or above (especially at the end of the workout).

3. Low blood sugar can make any workout a bad one. You may feel good at the start and suddenly feel like you have no energy. Every step seems to take a major effort. Read the chapter in this book about this topic.

4. Low motivation. Use the rehearsal techniques in the motivation section to get you out of the door on a bad day. The tips there have helped numerous exercisers turn their minds around—even in the middle of a workout.

5 Infection can leave you feeling lethargic, achy, and unable to exercise at the same pace that was easy a few days earlier. Check the normal signs (fever, chills, swollen lymph glands, etc.) and at least call your doctor if you suspect something.

6. Medication and alcohol, even when taken the day before, can leave a hangover that dampens a workout.

7. A slower start can make the difference between a good day and a bad day. When your body is on the edge of fatigue or other stress, it only takes a little bit too much exertion during a segment to push into discomfort or worse.

Cramps in the Muscles

At some point, most people who exercise experience cramps. These muscle contractions usually occur in the feet or the calf muscles and may come during the workout, or they are random. Most commonly, they will occur at night, or when you are sitting around at your desk or watching TV, reading, etc., in the evening.

Cramps vary in severity. Most are mild but some can grab so hard that they shut down the muscles and hurt when they seize up. Massage, and a short and gentle movement of the muscle can help to bring most of the cramps around. Odds are that stretching will make the cramp worse, or tear the muscle fibers.

Most cramps are due to overuse—exercising harder or longer than in the recent past, or continuing to exert your muscles to the limit, especially in warm weather. Look at the pace and duration of your workouts in your training journal to see if you have been increasing too much, or not slowing down in the heat.

- Continuous exercise increases cramping. Taking walk breaks more often can reduce or eliminate cramps. Many runners who used to cramp when they ran a minute and walked a minute, stopped cramping with a ratio of run 30 seconds and walk 30-60 seconds.

- During hot weather, a good electrolyte beverage during the day when not exercising can help to replace the salts that you body loses in sweating. Drinking a drink like Accelerade, for example, can help to top off these minerals when you drink about 6-8 oz every 1-2 hours.

- On very long hikes, walks or runs, however, the continuous sweating, especially when drinking a lot of fluid, can push your sodium levels too low and produce muscle cramping. If this happens regularly, a buffered salt tablet has helped greatly: Succeed is the best one I know of.

• Many medications, especially those designed to lower cholesterol, have as one of their known side effects, muscle cramps. Exercisers who use medications and cramp should ask their doctor if there are alternatives, in dosage, change of medication, or frequency.

Here are several ways of dealing with cramps:

1. Take a longer and more gentle warm-up.
2. Shorten your exercise segment.
3. Take more rest between exercise segments.
4. Shorten duration of segments or total workout on a hot/humid day.
5. Break your workout into two segments.
6. Look at any other activities that could be overusing the muscle and causing the cramps.
7. Take a buffered salt tablet at the beginning of your exercise.
8. Ease the pace—especially at the beginning of the workout.

Note: If you have high blood pressure, ask your doctor before taking any salt product.

Nausea or Diarrhea

Sooner or later, virtually every exerciser has at least one episode of nausea or diarrhea (N/D). It comes from the buildup of total stress. Most commonly, it is the stress of exercise on that day, due to the causes listed below. But stress can come from many unique conditions within the individual. Your body triggers the N/D to get you to reduce the exercise, which will reduce the stress. Here are the common causes.

1. *Working out too long or too hard* is the most common cause. Runners are confused about this, because the pace doesn't feel too fast in the beginning. Each person has a level of fatigue that triggers these conditions. Slowing down and

taking more rest between segments (runners take walk breaks more frequently) helps to manage the problem.

2. *Eating too much or too soon before working out.* Your system has to work hard when you're exercising, and when digesting food. Doing both at the same time significantly increases stress and can result in N/D. Having food in your stomach, in the process of being digested, is an extra stress and a likely target for elimination.

3. *Eating a high fat or high protein diet.* Even one meal that has over 50% of the calories in fat or protein can lead to N/D hours later.

4. *Eating too much the afternoon or evening, the day before.* A big evening meal will still be in the gut the next morning. When you bounce up and down during a workout, you add stress to the system often producing N/D.

5. *Heat and humidity are a major cause of these problems.* Some people don't adapt to heat well and experience N/D with minimal buildup of temperature or humidity. But in hot conditions, everyone has a core body temperature increase that will result in significant stress to the system—often causing nausea, and sometimes diarrhea. By slowing the pace, taking more rest between segments, and pouring water over your head, you can manage this better. The best time to exercise in warm weather is before the sun gets above the horizon—or in air conditioning.

6. *Drinking too much water before a workout.* If you have too much water in your stomach, and you are bouncing around, you put stress on the digestive system. Reduce your intake to the bare minimum. Most exercisers don't need to drink any fluid before a workout that is 60 minutes or less.

7. **Drinking too much of a sugar/electrolyte drink.** Water is the easiest substance for the body to process. The addition of sugar and/or electrolyte minerals, as in a sports drink, makes the substance harder to digest for many exercisers. During a workout (especially on a hot day) it is best to drink only water. Cold water is best.

8. **Drinking too much fluid too soon after a workout.** Even if you are very thirsty, don't gulp down large quantities of any fluid. Try to drink no more than 6-8 oz, every 20 minutes or so. If you are particularly prone to this N/D, just take 2-4 sips, every 5 minutes or so. When the body is very stressed and tired, it's not a good idea to consume a sugar drink. The extra stress of digesting the sugar can lead to problems.

9. **Don't let exercise be stressful to you.** Some exercisers get too obsessed about getting their workout done at a specific pace. This adds stress to your life. Relax and let your exercise diffuse some of the other tensions in your life.

Headache

There are several reasons why exercisers get headaches during workouts. While uncommon, they happen to the average runner about 1-5 times a year—usually after the very long workouts. The extra stress that heat puts on the body can trigger a headache on a tough day—even considering the relaxation that comes afterward. Many exercisers find that a dose of an over-the-counter headache medication takes care of the problem. As always, consult with your doctor about use of medication. Here are the causes/solutions.

Dehydration—if you exercise in the morning, make sure that you hydrate well the day before. Avoid alcohol the evening before, if you run in the mornings and have headaches. Also watch the salt in your dinner meal the night before. A good sports drink like Accelerade, taken throughout the day the day before, will help to keep your fluid levels and your electrolytes "topped off". If you exercise in the afternoon, follow the same advice leading up to your workout.

Medications can often produce dehydration—There are some medications that make exercisers more prone to headaches. Check with your doctor.

It's too hot for you—work out at a cooler time of the day (usually in the morning before the sun gets above the horizon). During a hot workout, pour water over your head.

Pushing the pace—start all workout segments more slowly, rest more during the segments

Exercising longer than you have in the recent past—monitor your time spent in workouts and don't increase more than about 15% further than you have run on any single workout in the past week.

Low blood sugar level—be sure that you boost your BSL with a snack, about 30-60 min before your workout. If you are used to having it, caffeine in a beverage can sometimes help this situation also.

If prone to migraines—generally avoid caffeine, and try your best to avoid dehydration. Talk to your doctor about other possibilities.

Watch your neck and lower back—If you have a slight forward lean as you run or walk and other exercise modes, you can put pressure on the spine—particularly in the neck and lower back.

Should I Exercise when I Have a Cold?

There are so many individual health issues with a cold that you must talk with a doctor before you exercise when you have an infection. Usually you will be given the OK to gently exercise. Check with the doctor.

Lung infection—don't work out! A virus in the lungs can move into the heart and kill you. Lung infections are usually indicated by coughing—but check this out.

Common Cold? There are many infections that initially seem to be a normal cold but are not. At least call your doctor's office to get clearance before exercising. Be sure to explain how much you are working out, and what, if any, medication you are taking.

Throat infection and above—most exercisers will be given the OK, but check with the doc.

Street Safety

Each year several runners or walkers are hit by cars when exercising. Most of these are preventable. Here are the primary reasons and what you can do about them.

1. *The driver is intoxicated or preoccupied by cellphone, etc.*

   Always be on guard—even when walking/running on the sidewalk or pedestrian trail. Many of the fatal crashes occurred when the driver lost control of the car, and came up behind the runner, on the wrong side of the road. I know it is wonderful to be on "cruise control" in your right brain, but you can avoid a life threatening situation if you will just keep looking around, and anticipate.

2. *The runner/walker dashes across an intersection against the traffic light.*

   When running or walking with another person, don't try to follow blindly across an intersection. Pedestrians who quickly sprint across the street without looking are often surprised by cars coming from unexpected directions. The best rule is the one that you heard as a child: When you get to an intersection, stop. Never assume that somone ahead of you is watching out for your safety.

3. *Sometimes, runners/walkers wander out into the street as they talk.*
One of the very positive aspects of social exercise becomes a negative one, in this case. Yes, chat and enjoy time with your friends. *But every exerciser in a group needs to be responsible for his or her own safety, footing, etc.* The biggest mistake I see is that those at the back of a group assume that they don't have to be concerned about traffic at all. This lack of concern is a very risky situation.

- In general, be ready to save yourself from a variety of traffic problems by following the rules below and any other that apply to specific situations. Even though the rules below seem obvious, many runners/walkers get hit by cars each year by ignoring them.
- Be constantly aware of vehicular traffic, at all times.
- Assume that all drivers are drunk or crazy or both. When you see a strange movement by a car, be ready to get out of the way.
- Mentally practice running for safety. Get into the practice of thinking ahead at all times, with a plan for that current stretch of road.
- Run/walk as far off the road as you can. If possible run on a sidewalk or pedestrian trail.
- Walk or run facing traffic. A high percentage of traffic deaths come from those who are going with the flow of traffic, and do not see the threat from behind.
- Wear reflective gear at night. I've heard the accounts and this apparel has saved lives.
- Take control over your safety—you are the only one on the road who will usually save yourself.

Dogs

When you enter a dog's territory, you may be in for a confrontation. Here are my suggestions for dealing with your "dog days":

1. There are several good devices that will help deter dogs: an old fashioned stick, rocks, and some electronic signal devices, pepper spray. If you are in a new area, or an area of known dogs, I recommend that you have one of these at all times.

2. At the first sign of a dog ahead, or barking, try to figure out where the dog is located, whether the dog is a real threat, and what territory the dog is guarding.

3. The best option is to walk or run a different route.

4. If you really want or need to go past the dog, pick up a rock if you don't have another anti-dog device.

5. Watch the tail. If the tail does not wag, beware.

6. As you approach the dog it is natural for the dog to bark and head toward you. Raise your rock as if you will throw it at the dog. In my experience, the dog withdraws about 90% of the time. You may need to do this several times before getting through the dog's territory. Keep your arms up.

7. In a few cases you will need to throw the rock, and sometimes another if the dog keeps coming.

8. In less that 1% of the hundreds of dog confrontations I've had, there is something wrong with the dog, and it continues to move toward you. Usually the hair will be up on the dog's back. Try to find a barrier to get behind, yell loudly in hopes that the owner or someone will help you. If a car comes by,

try to flag down the driver, and either stay behind the car as you get out of the dog's territory, or get in the car for protection if that is appropriate.

9. Develop your own voice. Some use a deep commanding voice, some use a high pitched voice. Whichever you use, exude confidence and command.

The Clothing Thermometer

After years of coaching exercisers in various climates, here are my recommendations for the appropriate clothing based upon the temperature. The first layer, since it will be next to your skin, should feel comfortable, with technical fibers, to move the moisture away from your skin. You may have to resist the temptation to buy a fashion color, but function is most important. Actually, more and more technical garments are attractively presented. As you try on the clothing in the store, watch for seams and extra material in areas where you will have body parts rubbing together thousands of times during a walk (armpit, between legs).

Cotton is not a good fabric for those who perspire a great deal, as it absorbs the sweat, holding it next to your skin, increasing the weight you must carry during exercise. Garments made out of fabric labeled Polypro, Coolmax, Drifit, etc., can retain enough body heat to keep you warm in winter, while releasing the extra amount. By moving moisture to the outside of the garment, these technical fabrics help you stay cooler in summer, while avoiding the winter chill.

Temperature	What to wear
60° F and above (14° C +)	Tank top or singlet, and shorts
50° to 59° F (9° to 13° C)	T-shirt and shorts
40° to 49° F (5° to 8° C)	Long sleeve light-weight shirt, shorts or tights (or nylon long pants), mittens and gloves
30° to 39° F (0° to 4° C)	Long sleeve medium weight shirt, and another T shirt, tights and shorts, socks or mittens or gloves and a hat over the ears

JEFF & BARBARA GALLOWAY

20° to 29° F (-4° to -1° C)	Medium weight long-sleeve shirt, another T shirt, tights and shorts, socks, mittens or gloves, and a hat over the ears
10° to 19° F (-8° to -5° C)	Medium weight long-sleeve shirt, and medium/heavy weight shirt, tights and shorts, nylon wind suit, top and pants, socks, thick mittens and a hat over the ears
0° to 9° F (-12° to -9° C)	Two medium or heavyweight long-sleeve tops, thick tights, thick underwear (especially for men), medium to heavy warm up,gloves and thick mittens, ski mask, a hat over the ears, and Vaseline covering any exposed skin.
-10° to 15°F (-18° to -13°C)	Two heavyweight long-sleeve tops, tights and thick tights, thick underwear (and supporter for men), thick warm up (top and pants),mittens over gloves, thick ski mask and a hat over ears, Vaselinecovering any exposed skin, thicker socks on your feet and otherfoot protection, as needed.
-20° both C & F	Add layers as needed or arrange shoes and clothing in front of the fire.

What Does the Research Say?

"For every hour you exercise, you will statistically add two hours to your lifespan."

"The notion that sports and recreational activities cause an inevitable wear on the joints just does not hold up when the scientific studies are evaluated. Few competitive, or recreational long distance runners suffer severe joint injuries and many regular runners can recall how long and how often they have run." Ross Hauser, M.D, and Marion Hauser M.S.R.D. as quoted in Dr. Larry Smith's website.

The evidence is growing that exercise will bring quality to your life, increase longevity and will not harm your joints—when done correctly. But every year I hear statements from uninformed doctors who are prejudiced against running, don't read the research, and who mistakenly maintain that humans were not designed for certain exercises—especially running. This chapter is your guide to the research, so that you can decide.

It's my opinion, and that of many medical experts, that most people will maintain their cardiovascular system better and suffer less joint damage by regularly and gently running and walking. During a clinic on his research findings (listed below), leading researcher Dr. Paffenbarger stated that for every hour you exercise, you can expect to have your life extended by 2 hours. That's a great return on investment!

But those who choose to push into speedwork, run too much or too fast for their current ability can cause orthopedic problems. Because there are many individual differences, especially during the aging process, you should find the medical experts in the areas that are important to you, and stay in touch about any problems that come up. You'll find suggestions in this book about "early warning" tests that can show potential problems, and how to choose doctors who are supportive of running and exercise. Consult your medical team on all medical issues.

Humans were designed for long distance running—and walking In the Journal NATURE, November 2004, Daniel Lieberman (Harvard), and Dennis Bramble (Univ. of Utah) state that fossil evidence shows that ancient man ran long distances. These experts and others point to the ancient bio mechanisms of the ankle, Achilles, buttocks, and many other components which are running specific adaptations. According to the extensive research of these scientists and others, one can say that humans were born to run, that covering long distances was a survival activity, and that body and mind are designed to adapt to gentle and regular walking/running. Some experts believe that ancient human ancestors ran before they walked.

Older runners can improve faster than younger runners. "You can maintain a very high performance standard into the sixth or seventh decade of life", said Dr. Peter Jokl, British Journal of Sports Medicine August 2004 (reported in MSNBC.com). This study found that runners over 50 years old improved their times in the NYC Marathon more than runners in younger age groups.

Exercise Prolongs Life
Living longer is related to the number of calories burned per week. Dr. Ralph Paffenbarger conducted a highly acclaimed and comprehensive study for the US Public Health Service, started in the 1960's. Results have been published in the Journal of the American Medical Association, April 1995 (co-authored by Doctors Lee and Hsieh). The conclusion: as the amount of exercise increases, rates of death from all major causes are reduced. Those who exercise more can statistically predict that they will live longer than they would when sedentary or with minimal exertion. His extensive research has also shown that the more calories burned, the greater the benefit.

Starting exercise after the age of 60 can lengthen life. Dr. Kenneth Cooper, founder and director of the Cooper Clinic and the Cooper Institute of Aerobic Research, has volumes of research on various aspects of this topic. Findings also reveal that men of all ages who exercise regularly experience a 60% reduction in heart attacks, while women show a 40% reduction.

Breast cancer reduced in females who regularly exercised during the childbearing years. This was reported in the Journal of the National Cancer Institute.

Older runners reduced their risk of heart disease, as they increased weekly mileage. Research in the National Runners Health Study shows that as runners increase their weekly mileage, they experience a reduced ratio of total cholesterol to the "bad" HDL cholesterol. Higher mileage runners also reduce systolic blood pressure, while cutting down on waist and hip fat. The reduction in HDL among those running 40+ miles per week, represents a 29-30% reduction in heart attack risk.

Exercise reduced death rate in women. This was the conclusion by Lissner et al, in the American Journal of Epidemiology (Jan 1996), from an extensive study of Swedish women. The researchers also found that reducing physical activity increased risk of death. Sherman et al found that the most active women exercisers cut their death rate by one third (American Heart Journal, Nov 1994).

Colon cancer and GI hemorrhage decreased by regular exercise. Several studies show a 30% reduction of colon cancer among regular exercisers. Gastrointestinal hemorrhage research is reported by Pahor et al (JAMA Aug 1994).

Better thinking: Spirduso (Physical Fitness, Aging, and Psychomotor Speed: a review in Journal of Gerontology 1980) found that those who regularly exercised performed better on tests of cognitive functioning.

Less depression, better attitude: Eysenck et al (Adv Behav Res Ther 1982) found that active folks were more likely to be better adjusted compared with sedentary individuals. Folkins et al (American Journal of Psychology 1981) showed that exercise improves self-confidence and self-esteem. Weyerer et al reported that patients who exercised and were given counseling did better than with counseling alone (Sports Medicine, Feb 1994). Blumenthal et al (Journal of Gerontology 1989) found that exercise training reduces depression in healthy older men, and Martinsen et al (British Medical Journal 1985) found exercise very effective in populations with major depression. Camancho et al (American Journal of Epidemiology 1991) found that newcomers to exercise were at no greater risk for depression than those who had exercised regularly.

Running and Joint Health

Running does not predispose joints to arthritis Dan Wnorowski, MD, has written a paper which reviews research on the effects of running and joint health. He believes that the "majority of the revelant literature during the past decade" on this topic finds little or no basis that running increases arthritis risk. Wnorowski goes on to say that a recent MRI study indicates that the prevalence of knee meniscus abnormalities in asymptomatic marathon runners is no different than sedentary controls.

- "Studies have shown that joint nourishment is entirely based upon keeping joints in motion"
  Charles Jung, MD from Group Health Cooperative website.

- "We don't see marathon runners having more joint injuries than sedentary folks. Simply put, active people have less joint injury."
  P.Z. Pearce, MD from Group Health Cooperative website.

- "Running offers up to 12 year's protection from onset of osteoarthritis," BBC website 16 Oct 2002.

- "Painless running or other activities which are aerobic and make you fit help keep you vigorous for longer." Professor Jim Fries, Stanford University (commenting upon results of his research at Stanford on aging exercisers).

- "Inactivity was once thought to prevent arthritis and protect fragile arthritic joints from further damage. More recent research has demonstrated the opposite." Benjamin Ebert, MD, PhD, as quoted in Dr. Larry Smith's website.

Older runners reported pain and disability only 25% as often as those who didn't run. A study conduced by Fries, et al.

"Running or jogging does not increase the risk of osteoarthritis even though traditionally we thought it was a disease of wear and tear." Dr. Fries, from his study.

"Reasonably long-duration, high mileage running need not be associated with premature degenerative joint disease of the lower extremities." Panush et al, "Is Running Associated with Degenerative Joint Disease?"JAMA 1986. Subjects were at least 50 years old, mean # of years running: 12, mean weekly mileage 28.

No increase in degenerative joint disease in runners. "Competitive sports increase joint risk—but running risk is low". Lane, et al, "Risk of Osteoarthritis(OA) With Running and Aging: Five Year Longitudinal Study". Studied runners 50-72 years old. Findings were similar to the conclusions of a study in 1989.

"Running seems to be devoid of adverse effects leading to knee degeneration, compared with other sports." Kujala et al, "Knee Osteoarthritis in Former Runners, Soccer Players, Weight Lifters, and Shooters," Arthritis & Rheumatism, 1995.

"Runners averaging 66 years of age have not experienced accelerated development of radiographic OA (Osteo-Arthritis)

of the knee compared with nonrunner controls" Lane et al, Journal of Rheumatology 1998.

"Older individuals with OA of the knees (not endstage) benefit from exercise." Ettinger et al, JAMA 1997.

"Little or no risk of OA with lifelong distance running" Konradsen et al, (AJSM 1990) studied a group that tends to abuse the orthopedic limits (former competitive runners) who ran 20-40 km per week for 40 years. Other interesting studies include Lane et al, JAMA 1989, Kujala et al, Arthritis & Rheumatism 1995.

Note: The American Heart Association has a wonderful document that details the varied and significant benefits from exercise, citing 107 research sources. You can search for this on the internet under "AHA Medical/Scientific Statement".

Products that Enhance Exercise

For more information on these, visit *www.JeffGalloway.com* or www.phidippides.com

Other Galloway Books: training schedules, and gifts that keep on giving—even to yourself
(Order them, autographed, from *www.JeffGalloway.com*)

More Recent Publications*
***Running Until You're 10**0* In the chapter on joint health, you'll see in the research studies that runners have healthier joints than sedentary folks. In the chapter on the researched health benefits of exercise, an expert on longevity says that for every hour we exercise we can expect to get back 2 hours of life extension. Among the heroes section is an 85 year old who recently finished his 700th marathon and will do 29 more this year. There are

nutrition suggestions from Nancy Clark, training adjustments by decade, and many other helpful hints for running past the century mark.

Fit Kids—Smarter Kids This is a handbook for parents, teachers, youth leaders in how to lead kids into fitness that is fun. A growing number of studies are listed that document how kids who exercise do better in academics, and in life. Nancy Clark gives tips on what to eat, and there's a chapter on childhood obesity—with the hope that others, like the author (a former fat kid) can turn things around. There are resources, successful programs, inspirational stories and much more.

A Woman's Guide To Running & A Woman's Guide to Walking By Barbara and Jeff Galloway. The section on woman-specific issues makes this book unique: pregnancy, menstrual issues, bra-fitting, incontinence, osteoporosis, inner organs shifting, menopause and more. There's a section for the unique problems of the "fabulously full figured" runners. Nutrition, fat-burning, motivation, starting up, aches and pains—all are covered in the book. There's also a section in each book written by famous sports nutritionist Nancy Clark.

Walking: Walkers now have a book that explains the many benefits, and how to maximize them, with training programs for 5K, 10K, Half and Full Marathons. There is resource information on fat burning, nutrition, motivation and much more.

Getting Started: This is more than a state-of-the-art book for beginners. It gently takes walkers into running, with a 6 month schedule that has been very successful. Also included is information on fat burning, nutrition, motivation, and body management. This is a great gift for your friends or relatives who can be "infected" positively by running.

A Year-Round Plan You'll find daily workouts for 52 weeks, for three levels of runners: to finish, maximize potential, and improve time. It has the long runs, speed sessions, drills, hill sessions, all listed in the order needed to do a 5K, 10K, Half and Marathon during one year. Resource material is included to help with many running issues.

Galloway's Book On Running 2nd Edition: This is the best-seller among running books since 1984. Thoroughly revised and expanded in 2001, you'll find training programs for 5K, 10K, Half Marathon, with nutrition, fat burning, walk breaks, motivation, injuries, shoes, and much more. This is a total resource book.

Galloway Training Programs This has the information you need to train for the classic event, the marathon. But it also has schedules for Half Marathon and 10 Mile. New in 2007, this has the latest on walk breaks, long runs, practical nutrition, mental marathon toughness and much more.

Half Marathon This new book provides highly successful and detailed training schedules for various time goals, for this important running goal. Information is provided on nutrition, mental preparation, fluids, race day logistics & check list, and much more.

Testing Yourself: Training programs for 1 mile, 2 mile, 5K, and 1.5 mile are detailed, along with information on racing-specific information in nutrition, mental toughness, running form. There are also some very accurate prediction tests that allow you to tell what is a realistic goal. This book has been used effectively by those who are stuck in a performance rut at 10K or longer events. By training and racing faster, you can improve running efficiency and your tolerance for waste products, like lactic acid.

5K-10K Whether you want to finish with a smile on your face, or have a challenging time goal in mind, this book is a total resource for these distances. There are schedules for a wide range of performances, how to eat, how to predict your performance, how long and how fast to run on long runs, drills to improve form and speed training. There is extensive information on mental preparation, breaking through barriers, practical nutrition and more.

Jeff Galloway's Training Journal

Some type of journal is recommended to organize, and track, your training plan. Jeff Galloway's Training Journal can be ordered from www.JeffGalloway.com, autographed. It simplifies the process, with places to fill in information for each day. There is also space for recording the unexpected thoughts and experiences that make so many runs come alive again as we read them.

Running Schools and Retreats: Jeff conducts motivating running schools and retreats. These feature individualized information, form evaluation, comprehensively covering running, nutrition, and fat burning.

Podfitness—coaching through the iPod

An extension of Jeff's training programs. He has teamed up with Podfitness.com to bring these workouts into your daily life. Now, you can have a custom program, during which Jeff coaches you through every training session on your iPod.

"My Podfitness training program is designed to reinforce what you've read here. Your program is designed expressly for you, and changes with you. You'll hear me throughout your workout, offering advice and encouragement. Plus, it plays your music in the background, which I think makes each run even more enjoyable." JG

Go to http://www.podfitness.com/jeffgalloway/ and they'll let you try it for free. I'm positive you'll be as impressed with it as I was, and that you'll become a better runner for it.

The Stick

This massage tool can help the muscles recover quicker. It will often speed up the recovery of muscle injuries or Iliotibial band injuries (on the outside of the upper leg, between knee and hip). This type of device can warm up the leg muscles and reduce the aggravation of sore muscles and tendons. By promoting blood flow during and after a massage, muscle recovery time is reduced.

To use "the stick" on the calf muscle (most important in running), start each stroke at the Achilles tendon and roll up the leg toward the knee. Gently roll back to the origin and continue, repeatedly. For the first 5 minutes a gentle rolling motion will bring additional blood flow to the area. As you gradually increase the pressure on the calf during an "up" stroke, you'll usually find some "knots" or sore places in the muscles. Concentrate on these as you roll over them again and again, gradually breaking up the tightness. See www.RunInjuryFree.com for more info on this.

Foam Roller—self massage for I-T Band, Hip, etc.
This cylinder of dense foam is about 6" in diameter and about one foot long. We've not seen any mode of treatment for Iliotibial band injury that has been more effective. For best effect, put the roller on the floor, and lie on your side so that the irritated I-T band area is on top of the roller. As your body weight presses down on the roller, roll up and down on the area of the leg you want to treat. Roll gently for 2-3 minutes and then apply more pressure as desired. This is actually a deep tissue massage that you can perform on yourself. For I-T band, we recommend rolling it before and after running. See www.RunInjuryFree.com for more info on this product.

Cryo-Cup—best tool for ice massage
Rubbing with a chunk of ice on a sore area (when near the skin) Is very powerful therapy. We know of hundreds of cases of Achilles tendon problems that have been healed by this method. The Cryo-Cup is a very convenient device for ice massage. The plastic cup has a plastic ring that sits on top of it. Fill it up with water, then freeze. When you have an ache or pain that is close to the skin, take the product out of the freezer, pour warm water over the outside of the cup to release it, and hold onto the plastic

handle like an ice "popsicle". Rub constantly up and down the affected area for about 15 minutes, until the tendon (etc.) is numb. When finished, fill the cup and place in the freezer. In my experience, rubbing with a plastic bag of ice—or a frozen gel product—does no good at all in most cases.

*YOU CAN DO IT—motivational audio CD

Put this in your car player as you drive to your run. You'll be motivated by the stories as you learn the strategies and methods that have allowed runners to deal with the negative messages of the left side of the brain—and push to their potential. (www.JeffGalloway.com)

Endurox Excel (pills)

Many runners over 50 years old have told us that they have noticed a significantly faster muscle rebound when using this product. An hour before a long or hard workout, Jeff takes two of these Excel pills. Among the antioxidants is the active ingredient from eleuthero: ciwujia. Research has shown that recovery time is reduced when this product is taken. We also use it when our legs have been more tired than usual for 2-3 days in a row.

Accelerade—best for hydration

This sports drink has a patented formula shown to improve recovery. Drinking it before and after prolonged, dehydrating workouts also helps to improve hydration. We recommend having a half gallon container of Accelerade in the refrigerator. Drink 4-8 oz every 1-2 hours, throughout the day. Best time to "top off" your fluid levels is within 24 hours before a long run. Prime time for replacing fluids is during the 24 hour period after a long run. Many runners have 32 oz or so in a thermos, for sipping during walk breaks in a prolonged speed training session. I suggest adding about 25% more water than recommended.

Research has also shown that drinking Accelerade about 30 min before running can get the body's startup fuel (glycogen) activated more effectively, and may conserve the limited supply of this crucial fuel.

Endurox R4—for recovery
This product has almost "cult following" status among runners. In fact, the research shows that the 4-1 ratio of carbohydrate to protein helps to reload the muscle glycogen more quickly (when consumed within 30 min of the finish of a hard or long workout. This means that the muscles feel bouncy and ready to do what you can do, sooner. There are other antioxidants in R4 that speed recovery. Discount available at www.JeffGalloway.com.

Your journal allows you to take control over the organization of your training components. As you plan ahead and then compare notes afterward, you are empowered to learn from your experience, and make positive changes.

Galloway PC Coach—interactive software
This software will not only set up a marathon training program, it will help you to stay on track. As you log in, you're told if your training is not what it should be for that day. Sort through various training components quickly, and often find reasons why you arc tired or have more aches and pains, etc.

Vitamins
I now believe that most runners need a good vitamin to boost the immune system and resist infection. There is some evidence that getting the proper vitamin mix can also speed recovery. The vitamin line I use is called Cooper Complete. Dr. Kenneth Cooper (founder of the Cooper Clinic and the Aerobics Institute), is behind this product. In the process of compiling the most formidable body of research on exercise and long-term health I've seen anywhere, he found that certain vitamins play important roles. Discount available at www.JeffGalloway.com.

Buffered Salt Tablets—to reduce cramping

If your muscles cramp on long or hard runs, due to salt depletion, this type of product may help greatly. The buffered sodium and potassium tablets get into the system more quickly. Be sure to ask your doctor if this product is OK for you (those with high blood pressure, especially). If you are taking a statin drug for cholesterol, and are cramping, it is doubtful that this will help. Ask your doctor about adjusting the medication before long runs.

CONTROL OVER PACE BY GPS AND OTHER DISTANCE-PACE CALCULATORS

There are two types of devices for measuring distance, and both are usually very accurate: GPS and accelerometer technology. While some devices are more accurate than others, most will tell you almost exactly how far you have run/walked. These will allow you to gain control over your pace—from the first 10th of a mile.

Freedom! With these devices, you can run/walk your long ones wherever you wish, instead of having to repeat a loop—just because it is measured. Instead of going to a track to do a "magic mile", you can very quickly measure your segments on roads, trails or residential streets.

Advisors:

Paula Bacon
John Cantwell, MD
Nancy Clark, RD
Terry Davis, MD
Julie Gazmararian, MPH, PhD
Nicole Hagedorn, DO, OB/GYN
Dave Hannaford, DPM
Ruth Parker, MD
Diana Twiggs, MD
Wendy Welch, MD

Photos & Illustration Credits:

Jeff Galloway

Jeff & Barbara Galloway
Women's Complete Guide to Running

2nd Edition
232 pages, full-color print
50 color photos, 5 charts
Paperback, $6^{1}/2$" x $9^{1}/4$"
ISBN: 978-1-84126-205-5
$ 16.95 US
£ 12.95 UK/€ 16.95

This is the book that will take any woman, at any level of fitness, into the running lifestyle. Jeff developed the run-walk method of training, and together with his wife Barbara he offers a step-by-step program specifically designed for the needs and concerns of women. All of the described programs and exercises can be incorporated into the busiest lifestyle – to improve attitude, relieve stress, and enjoy a greater sense of vitality.

Jeff Galloway
Running – Getting Started

3rd Edition
232 pages, full-color print
63 photos
Paperback, $6^{1}/2$" x $9^{1}/4$"
ISBN: 978-1-84126-242-0
$ 16.95 US
£ 12.95 UK/€ 16.95

"Running – Getting Started" will take anyone, at any level of fitness, into the running lifestyle. Jeff Galloway offers a step-by-step program that is easy to use and easy to understand. Included will be lots of tips on nutrition, staying motivated, building endurance, shoes, stretching and strengthening, and much more. Jeff Galloway has helped over 150,000 people into running while reducing or eliminating aches, pains, and injuries suffered during most training programs.

www.m-m-sports.com

America's No. 1 Running Book Author

Jeff & Barbara Galloway
**Women's Complete
Guide to Walking**

232 pages, full-color print
60 color photos
Paperback, 6¹/2" x 9¹/4"
ISBN: 978-1-84126-218-5
$ 16.95 US
£ 12.95 UK/€ 16.95

This book provides practical information on issues that are specific to women. There is also information on fat-burning, day-by-day schedules to get you into shape, motivation tips, and inspirational stories of women who have worked through major challenges in their lives, empowered by exercise. The nutrition section offers specific eating suggestions, with advice from highly recognized sports nutritionist Nancy Clark, RD. The information presented in this book is accessible and inspirational.

Jeff Galloway
Walking – The Complete Book

216 pages, full-color print
48 photos, 16 illustrations
Paperback, 5³/4" x 8¹/4"
ISBN: 978-1-84126-170-6
$ 17.95 US
£ 12.95 UK/€ 16.95

This book will motivate you to get moving, avoid aches and pains, and enjoy a more energetic life. Whether you are just starting to walk around the block, or have been active for years, "Walking – The Complete Book" has a world of information that will make you want to walk every day, as it helps you improve the experience. This book explains how to keep moving forward – for life.

The Sports Publisher

MEYER & MEYER Sport

MEYER
& MEYER
SPOR